The CIA's
Russians

The CIA's
Russians

John Limond Hart

Naval Institute Press
Annapolis, Maryland

Naval Institute Press
291 Wood Road
Annapolis, MD 21402

Library of Congress Cataloging-in-Publication Data
Hart, John Limond, 1920–
    The CIA's Russians / John Limond Hart.
    p. cm.
    Includes bibliographical references and index.
    ISBN 1-59114-352-7 (alk. paper)
    1. United States Central Intelligence Agency—Biography. 2. Defectors—
Soviet Union—Biography. 3. Spies—Soviet Union—Biography. 4. Espionage,
American—Soviet Union. I. Title.
    JK468.I6H375 2003
    327.1273047'092'2—dc21

                                                              2002156366

Printed in the United States of America on acid-free paper ∞
10 09 08 07 06 05 04 03   9 8 7 6 5 4 3 2
First printing

To my wife, Katharine,
my two daughters,
Lisa Hamilton and Cathy Michaels,
and my seven grandchildren

Contents

Foreword

Spies have fascinated novelists, journalists, and historians—and the reading public—for centuries. Using overtones of tragedy and heroics, and sometimes sordid cynicism, authors have tried to portray the successes, adventures, and human disasters associated with the ancient profession of espionage, while often indiscriminately blending fact and fiction. Unfortunately most books on this subject have been produced by people outside the intelligence profession, many of whom have drawn upon their imaginations to portray the pressures, temptations, and thrills of leading lives devoted to this frequently dangerous profession.

John Hart brings a new approach to the age-old search for understanding this subject—the professional intelligence operator who also is a scholar. Hart's rendering is no outsider's fantasy of what the life of a spy must be like; his depiction comes from many years of involvement in the recruitment, management, and sometimes even psychological counseling of real spies. After World War II Hart spent nearly twenty-five years directing CIA intelligence operations as chief in Korea, Thailand, Morocco, and Vietnam; managing agency operations against Albania, China, and Cuba; and for four years running all CIA operations in Western Europe. He has known firsthand the difficulties of penetrating Communist regimes' counterespionage defenses, and personally experienced the agony of betrayal by Soviet agents such as Kim Philby, the renegade Englishman who for many years masqueraded as a patriotic British intelligence officer.

I knew John as more than the prototype of the tough field operator. He also was a thoughtful student of espionage as a profession. In 1971, nearing the end of his active duty career with the CIA, he asked the then-director of Central Intelligence, Richard Helms, to allow him a year to study the personalities and circumstances that had led a number of Soviet citizens to spy on behalf of the United States. During that year John reviewed the details of a number of CIA-run espionage cases, each of whose massive files filled many four-drawer safes. These operational records were more than impersonal chronological documentation; they were deeply human accounts of the thoughts and emotions of men who had taken the risk of spying on behalf of the United States, all too often costing them their lives. John thus made an effort to grasp the human factors that had led to their commitment as spies, as well as to identify the qualities and vulnerabilities that might enable U.S. intelligence agencies to identify and work with others like them in the future. Intrigued by these unusual men, John took a master of arts degree in psychology in an effort to better comprehend the human relationship that must be forged between the spy and his foreign contact.

The result is a highly professional analysis of a relationship that has been left too long to novelists and sensational journalists. In this account John has distinguished the person who merely flees the oppressive atmosphere of his homeland from the opposite—the heroic, sometimes reckless individual who remains within the target country in order better to warn us of dangers facing our nation. He also examines the influence of the political atmosphere that, before the collapse of the Soviet Union, pervaded and still pervades its elite; he makes clear that it was not necessarily the proletariats of Russian society who spied against their homeland, but many who had successfully risen in the elite social structure. It is a permissible hypothesis that those of the latter category were in fact the forerunners of the much larger segments of society that have since risen to throw off Soviet dictatorship and take their place among the comity of free nations.

Looking ahead John recognized the development of improved relationships between the United States and the countries of the former Soviet Union and examined the question of the need for espionage in the area where it once flourished most actively.

William E. Colby
Former Director of Central Intelligence

Preface

Toward the end of 1971, after a quarter-century career in the Operations Directorate of the Central Intelligence Agency (CIA), including several overseas assignments as chief of station and a headquarters position as an area division chief, I made my way to the office of Richard Helms, at the time the director of Central Intelligence, to ask for an unusual assignment of my own devising. It seemed to me that none of us knew exactly why a very small minority of Soviet officials chose to work clandestinely for, or defect to, the West. Should we not make a more systematic effort to understand what led some to collaborate while others refused to consider any such act? Agents-in-place were, after all, the lifeblood of our then-highest-priority intelligence-collection program targeted at the Soviet Union, and we needed a better understanding of them.

I proposed to spend a year researching in depth a representative group of Soviet espionage cases handled by the agency. This research should be conducted, I suggested, in consultation with members of the agency's excellent psychological and psychiatric staffs in the hope of discovering some of the secrets and possible common denominators

behind the willingness of certain Soviets to spy on our behalf, whereas most were not so inclined. Helms agreed to my proposal.

Later, after several years of contented retirement in my quiet home
outside Washington, D.C., I was asked to abandon my retreat and
return to duty for a few months. I was told that the agency needed
someone to assess the complex and unpleasant case of a Soviet citizen,
Yuri Nosenko, who had been held in solitary confinement in the
United States for a prolonged period. It was thought that I might pos-
sess the necessary background, detachment, and objectivity to unravel the truth as to why a normally decent U.S. government organization
had held him for three years under the most debasing of circumstances. I seemed to be the obvious candidate in light of having undertaken my earlier research.

I spent six months working full-time, researching and studying the
Nosenko case. The end result was the total absolution of Nosenko
and, in 1978, a subsequent discussion of the case at an open hearing of
the U.S. House of Representatives Select Committee on Assassinations.

The result of these two separate research efforts is this book, as I
came to understand the complex motivations of those who have
found the resolution of their personal conflicts and compulsions in the
dangerous craft of espionage. What were my sources? Happily, they
were enormous and varied. I had direct access to CIA files on a number of Soviet cases, including those discussed herein. Among other
things these files contained transcripts, assessments, and intelligence
production records. One Soviet, Oleg Penkovsky, alone provided
some ten thousand pages of highly secret Soviet military documents,
plus an abundance of information about himself, his motivations, and
his occasional foibles. He knew when he began passing material to us
that he could not escape the Soviet Committee of State Security (KGB)
and that he would face a horrible death, but he never faltered in trying to lay bare the details of what was going on in the Kremlin.
Another more modest Soviet of peasant stock, Pyotr Popov, also con-

tinued to produce massive amounts of information despite the growing personal danger from the KGB. As for Nosenko, I had the opportunity to interview him personally, in addition to studying the contents of several filing cabinets of material concerning his case.

The careers of other Soviet citizens who betrayed their country on our behalf are studied in this volume, and even more who deserved mention but, since they were still active, would have been vulnerable if mentioned in this discussion. The pages that follow nevertheless give an adequate idea of how and why these unusual men chose the fatal trail that they knew could lead only to sorrow in the end.

In this book I have freely expressed myself—I hope without offense to any of the fine people with whom I worked for so long. This slight volume is, of course, far from being a definitive work on Soviet espionage. Yet I hope it may still prove valuable as an in-depth depiction of what went on in the minds of some unusual men who, seemingly driven by forces beyond their control, chose to become spies on our behalf.

Since most of the original materials on which this book is based remain classified by the CIA, I am not in a position to cite my references more precisely, as would be expected in a more typical scholarly work. For this I apologize.

The CIA's Publications Review Board has reviewed this manuscript and assisted in eliminating classified information. The board proffers no security objection to its publication but its review should not be construed as an official release of information, confirmation of accuracy, or endorsement of the views presented.

Acknowledgments

I wish to express my appreciation to the late Richard Helms for giving me the time, the unhindered access to sensitive materials, and the research, linguistic, and secretarial support to make possible much of the work reflected in this book. I also profited from having been recalled from retirement, some four years after ending my active service, to study the case of Yuri Nosenko. Furthermore, neither of these research projects would have been possible without the dedicated efforts of the research assistants, linguists, and secretaries who tirelessly supported both of these efforts and who must remain nameless.

More recently, Thompson Buchanan, a Soviet specialist now retired from the U.S. Foreign Service, helped me peer into the future to speculate on the need for espionage in the coming years. I am much indebted to him for his insights.

The CIA's
Russians

Prologue
From Ally to Enemy

It is 1950, the Holy Year, and the faithful have flocked from all over the world to Rome, the center of Christendom. I want to be inconspicuous, and the easiest way to move unnoticed among the crushing masses of tourists and pilgrims is to blend into the crowd. By 9:30 in the evening I maneuver my little Fiat sedan into Vatican Square and park among a number of other small cars full of chattering Italians, all of us facing the papal palace. I leave my car doors unlocked; I am expecting visitors. The sun has set and the street lights are on, but it could be midday judging by the throng steadily gathering to wait for His Holiness to appear in a window high up on the wall of the palace.

When the pope at last appears, exactly at the stroke of ten, the cacophony of voices in dozens of languages quickly dies down. Thousands of men and women quietly cross themselves. The small figure in white, magically backlit by the interior glow of the palace, raises his hand to bless the faithful. By now two well-dressed men have quietly joined me in my car, for this nightly event at the Vatican is the perfect occasion for an inconspicuous meeting with my Romanian associates, Ion and Toni, who are helping me plan an intelligence venture into their native land.

Suddenly seized by the incongruity of our situation, I turn to them and remark in Italian, "Does it occur to you that this is a strange place to be plotting an espionage operation?"

"But no!" exclaims Ion, a man to whom whimsy is totally foreign. "Ours is a sacred mission!" I suppose it is, this trade of ours—which the greatest of directors of the Central Intelligence Agency, Allen Dulles, liked to call "the craft of intelligence"—practiced in so many places across the world, during both peacetime and wartime, for good and for evil. And, I should add, for the most part in the conviction that what one does is right and necessary.

Necessary, yes, but not always well executed. The only experience our country had in the collection of foreign intelligence was gained during World War II. With the end of hostilities, however, the world situation changed so dramatically that the United States' intelligence-collection business was essentially starting from scratch. We were uncertain of how to go about our appointed tasks, and we all too often failed at them—as we did in the case of the Romanian operation which Ion, Toni, and I had so laboriously crafted.

In 1948 failure was the rule rather than the exception. In theory one collects intelligence about one's enemies, not about one's friends, but for a while after the war there was even confusion as to which countries fitted into which category. The Soviet Union had been our ally during the war but, by the time I applied for a job with the CIA in late 1947, countries all over the world (including China) had either shifted or were shifting from one part of the political spectrum to another. No wonder we were uncertain, sometimes feeling as Christopher Columbus might have felt had he noticed in mid-ocean that the Santa Maria was leaking badly and his compass was out of whack.

What eventually lighted our course was the rapidity with which the Soviet Union, as she drew her satellite countries about her like a woman husbanding her young, became our principal enemy in the world.

Rolling Back the Iron Curtain — The Albanian Tragedy

From the outset of my three years in Italy, 1948 to 1951, I was part of a major U.S. effort to "roll back the Iron Curtain." Albania happened to be my specialty, for the not very persuasive reason that I had lived there between the ages of five and nine. That little country was now considered important because to the policymakers it seemed a particularly vulnerable target for our nation's aggressive new anti-Communist crusade.

Why? Well, to its north and east Albania was surrounded by Yugoslavia, which even though it remained Communist had nonetheless severed its ties with the Soviet Union; we thought that the "Jugs" (as we called the Yugoslavs) would resist any attempt by the Soviets to come to Albania's aid when we attempted to overthrow Albania's dictator, Enver Hoxha.

To the south was Greece, the historical birthplace of democracy, whose border provided overland access to the tiny mountainous land that consisted of only some eleven thousand square miles. Moreover, although Albania itself was dominated by a fiercely Communist government, its population felt a strong link with the United States because hundreds of thousands of Albanians had emigrated to our country during the previous several decades. Though most stayed on American soil and became U.S. citizens, some did not, returning instead to their homeland as soon as they had accumulated a substantial nest egg. Nonetheless, even those who had returned considered themselves American as much as Albanian. Thus the United States had a special place in the hearts of these remarkable people, even among Albanians who had never been to our country.

My own memories of the land evoke a magical place full of tall, heavily armed tribesmen in costumes that had gone unchanged for centuries. In the shadow of the rocky inhospitable mountains Turkish mosques stood within sight of Roman ruins. Only two motor-driven vehicles existed in the capital when I lived there as a child, and even those two were not used much because distances were short. The streets thronged with people and heavily laden donkeys, all of them mixing and moving freely at the same deliberate pace, undisturbed by traffic. An occasional shot might ring out during the daylight hours, denoting the settlement of a blood feud, but the sound would cause little commotion; such matters were private affairs between families.

No wonder, then, that it seemed plausible to those in Washington that Albania's ruthless Communist regime—an economic shambles on the Stalinist model—would be vulnerable not only to espionage but to a later attempt to overthrow its poverty-stricken government. If the United States led by Dwight Eisenhower and John Foster Dulles were going to do more than merely "contain" Communism, Albania appeared a remarkably good place to start.

Unfortunately, the U.S. government was overly optimistic in its estimation of how to go about the as-yet-to-be-learned task of overthrowing a foreign government. Though America had proved its magnificent capabilities for conducting conventional warfare during World War II, in the aftermath of that success it lacked the quite different skills necessary to deal with ruthless and secretive Communist enemies. The Americans involved in the anti-Albanian effort, whether they were connected with the CIA, the military services, the State Department, or the White House, all took as their model the British and U.S. support of the French anti-Nazi resistance during World War II, assuming that an analogous effort could be mounted to unseat Communist governments in Eastern Europe. They forgot that we had no experience in combating such Soviet-backed governments—no experience for the simple reason that the Soviet Union had been our ally, not our adversary, during the recent war. We completely failed to grasp the difference between resistance in Western Europe against hard-pressed German occupation forces facing almost uniformly hostile populations, and the postwar situation in the newly established Communist bloc.

In the 1940s and 1950s the comparative weight of international numbers had been reversed. The ruthless Soviet occupation armies were in themselves overwhelmingly large and, moreover, were closely linked with the Communist East European internal security forces that on a day-to-day basis helped maintain the dominance originally achieved by Soviet arms. Our cardinal mistake was in approaching the problem of a Communist-dominated Eastern Europe in the postwar period as if it were analogous to the France of 1943–44. Even so, given the combination of Albania's unusual feelings toward America, its steeply mountainous terrain, and its fierce sense of independence, this little country might have proved itself a special case had it not been for one fatal factor of which at the time we had not the slightest inkling: there was a traitor in our midst. Our effort to liberate Albania by infiltrating chosen Albanians from the West was foredoomed to failure because we were being systematically and unremittingly betrayed by a man we mistakenly trusted.

Never having been the victim of perfidy in my four years of military service, I could hardly have expected to encounter it in a new profession whose activities were buttressed by the strictest attention to security and secrecy. I nevertheless could and did complain about a bizarrely overcomplicated bureaucracy in Washington that attempted to run two separate sets of operations simultaneously in Albania, each of which sometimes impinged dangerously on the other because of the small size of the country. Making coordination between them even more difficult, one group of operations was run out of a CIA office in Greece, while my operation was based in Italy. I did not worry much about what was being arranged in Athens because I had all the work I could handle in Rome.

As has been reported by others, the CIA's separate but "coordinated" covert action force working in Greece and targeted against Albania, was being jointly run with the British. Following the wartime precedent of close Anglo-American cooperation in France, this new arrangement involved sharing information about the targets and activities of the teams our two countries were to deploy covertly in Albania from Greece. This arrangement proved to be the undoing of the entire effort. "Overall coordination," which became a key concept in the Albanian program, was supposed to be ensured by liaison between CIA and British intelligence officers in Athens and Rome and particularly in Washington by CIA headquarters and a British intelligence liaison officer named Harold "Kim" Philby. During the period of 1949 through 1951, when the Albanian activities were at their height, Philby had full access to information about the operations of both nations while working closely with the CIA's James Angleton, who during some of the time in question worked as chief of operations before his appointment as head of a newly organized counterintelligence staff. In both capacities Angleton turned over to Philby all the proposed drop-zone coordinates in advance of the launching of U.S.-run Albanian agents controlled from both Italy and Greece. (Drop zones are carefully chosen areas into which persons or supplies are dropped using an airborne operation.)

Unfortunately, behind Philby's persuasive charm and seeming dedication to the Anglo-American cause there lurked our ruin: his primary loyalty was to the Soviet Union and the KGB. Much later it was revealed that he had passed all the information regarding both the U.S. and British operations directly to his Soviet masters, thus enabling them to warn the Communist Albanian government in advance of the exact locations of every airdrop. Though my experience led me to realize that Albanian Communist troops were sometimes slow to react, in due course they closed in to kill our emissaries.

On a personal level, those of us who had responsibility for enlisting the services of the Albanian agents, then training and launching them into their homeland, were psychologically devastated when we could not contact them by radio and gradually realized that they must have been arrested as soon as they landed. What had we done wrong? We analyzed and reanalyzed our procedures, all the while marveling at the efficiency of the Albanian security forces to preempt our actions. It never occurred to anyone in the CIA that the fate of our Albanian compatriots was determined by a suave British intelligence liaison officer who served as a direct channel to the Soviets.

It is interesting to recall that, many years later, the charming and pensive Jim Angleton said to me, "I always suspected there was something wrong with Philby." I question the accuracy of that off-the-cuff statement, for he certainly never communicated such suspicions to any of his colleagues, nor did he take any preventive action at the time.

Paper Mills and Fabrications

A steamy summer day in Washington. It is mid-1952, and by now I am working at CIA headquarters as chief of intelligence operations for Southeast Europe. My in box contains an elaborate plan for a "network" of espionage agents who would "cover" the entire Balkans for us. Whatever other problems might haunt the espionage trade, we were never at a loss to find volunteers eager to accept our money. Determining what they could offer in return was a separate matter.

The file describing this proposed network had reached Washington from Vienna, and much of it struck me as strangely familiar. No wonder. Austria's capital during the four-power occupation after World War II had become a sort of intelligence bazaar where refugees from all over Communist Europe eked out a usually meager living at every imaginable trade. The traffic in intelligence was certainly one of the more lucrative forms of "free enterprise." Unencumbered by ideological or moral bias, many of these intelligence imposters tried to satisfy both the Soviet hunger for information about the three Western Allies and the West's equal interest in the plans, intentions, and capabilities of the USSR and its immense new bloc. Neither side, Soviet or Allied, seemed to be very good at evaluating the "intelligence" it purchased, so the traffic went on merrily, despite the fact that much of the merchandise was simply concocted by agile minds fabricating whatever they thought would catch the fancy of potential customers.

I turned to my secretary and asked, "Didn't we recently get this same item from The Hague?" Once she produced a file, I knew my memory served me correctly. Another commercially oriented "paper mill" had entered the market on a mass-production basis and had sent out its public-relations broadside. I hoped that the various Allied headquarters and subheadquarters in Vienna were not spending their "confidential funds" for such trash, but could muster no optimism at the thought. I had just finished quashing a bogus Romanian enterprise that Paris had credulously bought into and felt certain that the market contained more.

THE KOREAN WAR—PHANTOM AGENTS AND A REAL DEFECTOR

The problem of bogus "intelligence" haunted and hobbled our operations for years, not only in Europe but in Asia as well, where I arrived in 1952 as chief in Seoul, South Korea. My first self-appointed task upon arriving there was to take a hard look at the miraculous achievements claimed by my predecessors. To do so I established a small team of the brightest young "case officers" available and tried to inculcate in them a deep skepticism that should be the quintessential intellectual armor of the intelligence specialist. Concerning everything they had heard and read since arriving in Korea, I required each of them to ask, "Why should I believe this?"

I had been warned that none of our American officers could speak Korean, though we did have one or two good interpreters. Because of this absence of linguistic skill, our much-vaunted "assets" were for the most part handled through Korean "principal agents" (PAs, in agency jargon). From the hands of these native intermediaries (who to me seemed more entrepreneurial than analytical once I made a point of meeting some of them personally) we received the ostensible product of their "networks" in enemy territory. My curiosity concerning their bona fides began with a few basic questions: How much money did they appear to have? What had their record been before they came to work for us? What evidence supported the belief that they actually had access to anyone in the North? The initial investigation, lasting some three months, was climaxed by submitting all the PAs to polygraph tests.

The results of our investigation surpassed our most pessimistic expectations: though much of the vivid reporting we received may have been fabricated by people living in Seoul, strong indications led us to acknowledge that some of it actually had come down, in already "finished" form, from Pyongyang (capital of the North). One particular report lives in my memory. It purported to be a recapitulation of all Chinese and North Korean units along the battle line, citing each unit's strength and numerical designation. Received from a Seoul network a year earlier, the report had attracted much favorable attention, and the J-2 of the U.S. Far East Command—located far away, in Japan—had described it in writing as "one of the outstanding intelligence reports of the war." In fact, however, some rather sophisticated analysis subsequently revealed that this report was a total fabrication, containing no valid information whatsoever.

Meanwhile, our investigation of the PAs in Seoul had also borne fruit of a sort—most of it rotten. Under systematic interrogation, enhanced by lengthy polygraph tests, all of the sellers had turned out to be nothing but con men who had for some time been living happily on generous CIA payments supposedly being sent to "assets" in North Korea. Almost every report we had received from these notional agents came from our enemies.

I left my job as chief, Korea, in late 1955. The situation had improved only in that our organization had become professionally skeptical. The enemy's security precautions were so stringent that we still did not have any intelligence agents located in the North. Fortunately, there were brighter times during those clear, cool, cloudless days when Seoul, despite its devastation, had its moments of redeeming beauty—and, on one particular occasion, great excitement. Shortly after nine one morning the military phone on my desk jangled, and my usually imperturbable secretary announced with a hint of exhilaration in her voice, "Colonel, a North Korean air force pilot has just landed a Soviet MIG [Mikoyan-designed fighter aircraft] at K-16!" K-16 was the U.S. military designation for the American air base on the outskirts of the South Korean capital, and for a few hours it was likely to be the focus of attention for the entire U.S. command structure, stretching from the Pentagon to the air base's commanding officer. Never before had the United States had possession of a MIG, though there had been a standing offer of a one-hundred-thousand-dollar reward payable to anyone who could provide us with one of these fearsome weapons. In the currency of the 1950s this amount (equal to perhaps a million of today's dollars) was a sum so large that few Koreans could even comprehend it. Yet the price was considered modest by the U.S. Air Force, so much had our pilots learned to fear this Soviet plane during the long duel in the skies over Korea. The pilot had threaded his way at low altitude through the hills north of Seoul and therefore had not been even visually detected until the plane—coming in counter to the traffic pattern—stopped nose-to-nose facing a U.S. fighter preparing for take-off. By the time my olive drab sedan with a big white star on the side driving at top speed reached the base, the MIG had been ringed protectively by U.S. military police. The pilot, in accordance with U.S. government policy, was to be taken into custody by the CIA.

"Will you shoot me?" he asked. One of the first obligations we had in such cases was to reassure these unusual men who had abandoned their Communist homelands and thrown themselves on our mercy; the act of defection, once accomplished, usually left them in a state of shock from which they only gradually recovered. Their depression was often deep enough to evoke totally unrealistic fears of cruelty and even death at our hands, whereas in reality, because of the precious information they were capable of giving, we were inclined to treasure and coddle them. They had no way of knowing that fact in advance, however, and always seemed to expect the worst.

Defectors are unusual people, but even by that standard this pilot was a special case. He had been raised in a North Korean community where there had long been Korean-speaking American Christian missionaries, and he remembered them as kind and helpful—just the opposite, indeed, of the stern and arbitrary Communist authorities he had encountered. He had, therefore, defected simply because he trusted Americans; he had no inkling of the monetary reward that awaited him until we eventually told him about it. Upon hearing the news his first reaction was to turn it down, and we found ourselves in the curious position of having to urge his acceptance. There was a substantial American press corps in South Korea, and we feared adverse publicity if we did not fully honor our commitment. Once the lieutenant reached the United States under CIA auspices, he used his money for a good education and eventually, as an American citizen, became a successful engineer.

Defection has many dimensions. It may express a politically motivated protest, may stem from disappointment at not being promoted, or can be triggered by conflict with a superior. Whatever its origin, however, it is to some degree an emotional trauma. Until my arrival in Korea in 1952 I had had so little experience with men who had rejected their own countries that I was unprepared for the attendant psychological difficulties the situation almost universally produced, and most of my CIA colleagues turned out to be no better prepared than I. It had not occurred to any of us that such apostasy, even for a man who hated his country's political system, carried with it not just a feeling of apprehension of an uncertain future but also quite often a lingering sense of guilt. One clue to the depth of these feelings was the defectors' verbosity, which seemed often in proportion to their ambivalent reactions to having deserted their homelands. Their shame, though never clearly admitted, gnawed so viciously at some of them that they had to talk, talk, talk simply because, in the process, they could build up a structure of justification for their desertion. Nothing so complicated ever marred the adjustment of this Korean lieutenant to his new life, but he was an exception because of his experience with the American missionaries.

SPIES VERSUS DEFECTORS

Defection is operating at its most complex level when it takes place secretly, with the defector continuing to feign loyalty to his country while reporting clandestinely to another government. It is a far cry from defecting purely and simply on the one hand, and on the other being willing to go to the extreme of spying on your own country, as the cases of Aldrich Ames, Robert Hanssen, and others have shown. Though it may give rise to varying degrees of psychological trauma, outright defection is, after all, at least physically safe. If defectors bring with them valuable information accumulated in the course of their military or civilian work, once they have made it available to their chosen country they generally become the carefully guarded wards of a grateful government. Witness the case of the CIA's Edward Lee Howard, now living in Moscow. In our own country, once granted asylum a defector is likely to be given a new name and perhaps a "legend," or false life history to conceal his past. Until he finds a way to earn a living, the defector receives American financial support.

Spies, on the other hand, have to remain in place because their value to their adopted country hinges on continuing their careers in either the military or civilian services of their native land. In the Communist countries, whose coverage, at least until the collapse of the Soviet Union, was traditionally the highest priority of U.S. intelligence, spies have been forever at risk since the secret transmission of intelligence from a foreign city such as Moscow to CIA headquarters is inevitably difficult to accomplish. In intelligence jargon, before the end of the Cold War countries like the Soviet Union were referred to as "denied areas," where active and highly efficient counterespionage organizations went all out to uncover and prevent U.S. intelligence gathering. In today's climate of incipient freedom, the spy's job must now be considerably eased though still a far cry from risk-free.

Well before anyone had heard of *glasnost,* many Soviet citizens defied the odds against them by taking the initiative in "offering" to spy for the United States. Given the efficiency of the KGB, clearly one of the most effective organizations of its kind in the world, it is ironic that so many of America's most effective spies during the Cold War were Soviet citizens. Why were these Soviets willing to take such a risk? Why spy on behalf of a country whose language most of them did not speak? And, by contrast, why have fewer people of other major nationalities—particularly those in Communist Asia—been willing to do the same? Those are some of the questions we shall consider later.

While doing so we must of course keep in mind that this is an era of rapid political change, and generalizations derived from past experience must for some time be subject to continual reexamination. It is perhaps doubtful that even the members of today's foreign intelligence and security services are themselves sure what the future holds. Nonetheless, in studying spies of the past we can be reasonably sure that our generalizations will apply also to those who elect to betray their countries in the future. Just as America's liberal democracy has produced persons such as the Walker family, Jonathan Pollard, Aldrich Ames, and Robert Hanssen, all of whom were anxious to spy against it, so there will continue to be citizens of the countries of the former Soviet Union and other areas anxious to do so against their own homelands.

A QUESTION OF CULTURAL DIFFERENCES

The most cogent question that springs to mind as a result of these ideas so far is, Why spy? Why even try to spy, if the results are as dismal as depicted here? One answer often proffered is that the years described were the "kindergarten" period of the CIA, during which we were trying to cope with situations far beyond our ken. Unfortunately, however, the same experiences were repeated from 1966 to 1968, when our agency was certainly well beyond its infancy. I was by then once again a chief of station, but this time at a location in another war zone: Vietnam. We had learned enough by the late 1960s for our primary focus to be on helping the non-Communist South Vietnamese to defend their country against the Communists of the North. Nonetheless, Washington expected us to attempt operations in the North and, perhaps because of false pride, we did not protest as strongly as we should have. Without describing the details of our failures, let me simply say that they were substantially parallel to those we endured in Korea, but worse in one major respect: we received little if any word from our agents once they arrived in North Vietnam, and thus had no indication whatever of their fates. They simply vanished, without even sending bogus messages, as their North Korean predecessors often had.

These new setbacks led us to wonder whether there were commonalities between the failures we experienced wherever we tried to penetrate Communist Asia. Did our lack of success in this area perhaps mean that it was psychologically more impenetrable by Europeans and Americans than were the Slavic countries? Was there a basic cultural factor involved in our successes in Eastern Europe that one did not find in the countries heavily influenced by Chinese civilization? Those questions can be tentatively answered with an anecdote that sheds more light than would hundreds of rambling pages on the psychology of East Asians. In 1967, on my last evening posted in Saigon and about to be medically evacuated, I called to my bedside the two faithful servants, man and wife, who had cared for me day and night, seven days a week, for two years. I made a simple, sincere speech to express my gratitude, while they stood silent, impassive, and motionless. When I had finished they remained mute, almost at attention, as if they were uncertain how to react. (It fleetingly occurred to me that perhaps they had never before been praised!) Then at last Mr. Tang, as if realizing he had to say *something* before withdrawing, rattled off a few short phrases in Vietnamese. His message, as translated, was simply, "It is a servant's duty to do what the master wishes." Tang and his wife then bowed and quietly withdrew. In their minds mastery was everything. But why should I be obeyed so unquestioningly by them, yet be unable to get a spy to follow our orders once he arrived in North Vietnam? Many of the agents we dropped in were no doubt captured, but it strained credulity to believe that the North Vietnamese were one hundred percent successful in rounding up *everybody* we had dropped in north of the battle line. As I lay in bed, waiting for departure, I could not take my mind off this question, one that had haunted me since my days in Korea. Obviously the money I paid Mr. and Mrs. Tang was no small consideration in generating loyalty. But the agents we sent north were much more generously paid, so financial reward was not a key factor. Did mastery, then, perhaps stem from being on the spot—from being seen and heard, and giving orders in person? Yes, I decided, at least in part. The traditionalists of the Asian world such as the Tangs unquestioningly obeyed those superordinate persons whose presence was tangible, and who were also fair and honest with them. By contrast, Asians with only a traditional education rarely seemed sophisticated enough to function on their own after receiving guidance from someone known only from

afar; a secular authority beyond sight and hearing was thus no authority at all. Religious and quasi-religious authority were more effective,
but even they were too intangible to be compelling unless reinforced
by graven images, repetitive rituals, incantations, shibboleths, and—
perhaps—uniforms.

Regrettably from the standpoint of an intelligence officer, such
concrete psychological reinforcements run counter to the principles of
secrecy, and in any case even the most ardent U.S. case officer would
find the fortification of prayer inappropriate in the clandestine world
of intelligence. In Asia, on the other hand, the Communists (and similar totalitarians) seemed able to produce charismatic secular leaders
whose ideology carried with it the force of religion, and the "faith" of
these leaders was backed by complex and ubiquitous Party organizations. The Party's omnipresence was such that its members could spy
on us in a way we could not spy on them.

Let these words not be taken as a caricature of the Korean or
Vietnamese peoples. I have the utmost admiration and liking for them
both. Nonetheless, they simply did not function as most Americans
do—a peculiarity that continued to elude our country's understanding
during two long wars.

THE MATTER OF MOTIVATION

We can now formulate our central question: Why did a considerable
number of individual Soviet citizens volunteer their services to the
United States and certain Western powers and, having done so, why
did they then spy successfully on their own countries? One of the
agreeable surprises for all of us in the intelligence business after the
end of World War II was the unforeseen number of important Soviet
officials, particularly from the security and intelligence services, who
secretly reported to us at great length and depth on their own countries' most confidential activities while remaining in their civilian or
military jobs, despite the fact that the Soviet authorities considered

America their "main enemy" and until relatively recently we reciprocated that sentiment. Nowhere in the world had people been more aware of the dangers of espionage than in the Soviet Union, where the government made a point of publicizing the severe sanctions meted out to those who betrayed the Motherland. Why, then, did certain Soviet citizens so recklessly defy the odds? This book will attempt to answer that question. In addition, in the epilogue we shall examine the question as to whether espionage targeted against the former Soviet empire still makes sense given developments since the collapse of the Soviet Union.

We begin with a humble man named Pyotr Popov, of whom we in the CIA might not have expected much but who surprised us all—or at least those few in the agency who had a glance at his prowess.

1
Pyotr Popov
The Tribulations of Faith

1953: A SOVIET VOLUNTEER IN VIENNA

On New Year's Day 1953 as he enters his car in the International Sector of occupied Vienna, a young American vice consul discovers an envelope addressed to the American high commissioner. Vienna is a city on edge, occupied militarily by the four powers who were Allies during the war. There is no longer any unity; everyone knows that the World War II "alliance" has become a fiction and the subject of sick humor. "What is a war hero?" Austrians ask bitterly. To which the answer is, "Two Russians and a liter of vodka!" The aging and increasingly eccentric Stalin still rules; the Soviet Zone is rigorously separated from the areas designated for the French, British, and U.S. forces. On the other hand the so-called International Sector is a carefully delimited district where people of all nationalities are free to mix, however uneasily.

Cautiously opening the envelope, the vice consul finds a note written in Russian dated 28 December 1952. Once translated it appeared to be a muted plea for help:

I am a Soviet officer. I wish to meet with an American officer with
the object of offering certain services. Time: 1800 hours. Date: 1
January 1953. Place: Plankengasse, Vienna 1. Failing this meeting,
I will be at the same place, same time, on successive Saturdays.

Delivering that letter to a U.S. citizen was only the first of many
risks Maj. Pyotr Semyonovich Popov (soon to be Lieutenant Colonel
Popov) was to take over the next six years while assigned to Soviet
headquarters in Vienna. It was far from being his last dangerous gamble but, as Popov later remarked, "He who does not make any mistakes is not working!"

The Plankengasse "contact" with an American took place on the
following Saturday, as scheduled. Since Plankengasse was a public
street the meeting was kept brief so as not to attract attention. The
many lengthier meetings that followed, however, were conducted in
the small apartments of somber old gray buildings where, as if to epit-
omize the atmosphere of postwar Vienna, the furniture was stiffly formal yet threadbare. A Russian-speaking CIA case officer interviewed
the tense young man who, though less than thirty years old, was
already a major and claimed he would soon be promoted to lieutenant
colonel. The basic facts about him were soon verified because he had
documents to prove them. Nevertheless, Popov was obviously ill at
ease, and his replies to questions were at first short and curt.

As the two men came to know each other better, the reason for
Pyotr's nervousness became evident. Worldly he was not; he had never
known a foreigner before, and was unsure of how to deal with one.
What little the Soviet command told its officers about Americans was
unfavorable, and even though these strangers seemed pleasant enough
as they chatted and laughed while walking down the streets, the
young Russian was on his guard. Of only one thing was he certain:
Americans had lots of money. That belief was an item of faith within
the Soviet occupation forces.

What else did the Americans who came to know Popov learn about him? Of peasant stock, he was well educated for a person of his generation and background, but conversation with him produced no indication that he had ever read a book or on his own initiative taken any action to broaden his horizons. As was true for millions like him, the war had largely defined his life. His approach to one American picked at random was thus the first overt expression of his unrest and desire to determine his own destiny.

Given such a background, Popov was not perceived to be a key Soviet player in the Four Power Occupation of Austria. Yet, considering the ever-present tension between the Western Allies and the Russians that hung like a dark cloud over the supposedly joint administration of conquered Austria, for the CIA to have even a medium-level source operating within the Soviet general headquarters was bound to be of great value. This supposition was fully justified by future events, for relations between the four powers occupying the country remained tense, even bellicose, until they all left in 1955. Until then the continued threat of serious consequences resulting from mutual misunderstandings and drastically different political goals persisted.

East-West Tensions

The basis of tension between the West and the Soviets puts Popov's usefulness into perspective. Popov's first move in offering his services in Vienna took place some seven and a half years after the German high command signed an act of military surrender in Berlin on 7 May 1945, but that signature did not guarantee a secure peace. Indeed, from the beginning a considerable degree of hostility, much of it ideologically based, was inevitably present between the two sides of the alliance. As a U.S. Army captain I personally remember one Soviet division commander, with whom I was in liaison in Eastern Germany in 1945, threatening to shoot any American officer (presumably other than me) who might venture across the international boundary into his zone—and there were times when his obvious hatred of us left me far from confident of my own immunity. He may have been an extreme example, but his attitude mirrored the tone of U.S.-Soviet relations at the end of the war.

Major disagreements between the two sides had quickly taken shape in northern Germany, especially in and around Berlin. By May 1945 rapid advances had closed the physical gap between Western and Soviet forces. Proximity did not bring unity of purpose, however; and if anything it only increased hostility. Neither side had an even minimal level of trust in the other, despite General Eisenhower's vigorous efforts to establish harmony. Stemming in part from the sheer scale of military forces stationed in Europe, the problem was a type never before encountered by any of the senior commanders involved. As hundreds of thousands of heavily armed and aggressive (though theoretically allied) troops closed in on each other from both West and East, there existed vast room for misjudgment on the part of individual officers. Both the Western and Russian invasion forces, each in constant forward motion, functioned under complex but necessarily permissive command systems. On the Allied side, as orders filtered down through several echelons from Eisenhower's supreme headquarters to troops in the forward lines, a little of the sense and substance of the commander's desires was lost along the way. The same problem no doubt existed among the Russians, exacerbated by the fact that in both cases hostility against both the Allies and Germany began at the top, with Stalin.

The situation created infinite opportunities for misunderstanding, and sometimes accidental conflict. On one occasion, before we believed the Russian Army was near our area, I remember having gone far beyond the American lines on a reconnaissance mission to Chemnitz (under Communist rule known for many years as Karl–Marx–Stadt), in search of railway maps necessary for the evacuation of thousands of non-Communist refugees who had sought asylum from the Americans. Having just rescued them from a bunker harboring members of the German garrison, I emerged from their last redoubt only to be unpleasantly surprised by the arrival of a Russian armored force that promptly opened fire on my driver and me. Only the presence of mind of Sgt. Ethan Allan Webster, who had kept the engine running in our jeep, enabled us to beat a quick and prudent retreat.

The first major crisis in Soviet-Western relations came when the two sides closed in on each other in North Germany. Hitler's troops began to display a natural preference for surrendering to American or British commanders. The Russians, of course, took strong exception to the progress of events, though they had only themselves to blame since they seemed never to have heard of the Geneva Convention on the treatment of prisoners of war. Eisenhower ordered Western troops to block the approach of any German forces to our lines.[1]

The matter of Russian-Western relations was even more confused in Austria. The West had taken a benevolent attitude toward that country, on the grounds that it had become part of Nazi Germany only as a result of Hitlerian conquest. On the other hand, the Russians took no such charitable view. Having reached Austria first, they quickly occupied as much of the small land as they could, including Vienna, the nation's capital and home to more than one-fifth of the country's total population. The Russians then carried off considerably more industrial equipment "reparations" than had been foreseen in Allied agreements.[2]

Faced with U.S. and British protests, the Russians were not at all obliging. Under the aegis of the Soviet military commander in chief they organized a provisional government for Austria that had a Socialist president but two Communists in other key positions. The U.S. and British governments understandably began to wonder whether the Russians were planning to establish yet another East

European satellite. Fortunately, the new government turned out to be a pleasant surprise. More pro-Western than expected, Austria, though still subject to the four-power occupation, became a unified, democratically run country. The Americans and Russians nevertheless continued to watch each other nervously, always fearful of a double cross, until the occupation ended in 1955.

Given this tense situation it is understandable that Popov, a senior officer in the Soviet headquarters in Austria, was considered important to the CIA since he could provide early warning of hostile intentions on the part of the large and somewhat unpredictable Soviet Army in Europe. In the end the Russians exercised more restraint than the Allies at first had reason to expect, but Popov nonetheless provided important information that reassured the Western powers of the Russians' intent to adhere, even if somewhat grudgingly, to the four-power agreement on Austria.

POPOV'S EARLY LIFE

Why did an apolitical man like Pyotr Popov volunteer his services to U.S. intelligence? For purposes of this inquiry the spy's motivation (rather than the information he produced) is the central question, and the answer is more complex than might at first be expected. Like many of the men who labored quietly in the gray mists of espionage, Popov cannot be said in the long run to have had one single, simple motive for betraying his country. Moreover, the internal forces compelling him to cooperate with us became increasingly complex as time wore on.

To start at the beginning, we must naturally ask whether Popov volunteered his services because of his feelings of anti-Communism. The answer is categorically "No!," for the simple reason that he did not think in doctrinal terms. Instead, he was reacting in a highly personal way to the unpleasant impact that the Communist system had on his family, at first having no understanding of the political and economic alternatives offered by the West. How, then, does one sum up his motivation? Hatred of superiors? Loneliness? Confusion? A need for moral support? The answer to each question is maddeningly similar to the one given for every other question: only partly. Like other individuals we may encounter in studies of espionage, Popov's clandestine career as a U.S. intelligence agent was the product of complex and subtle multiple motivations.

The one thing that can be said about Popov with certainty is that wherever he found himself, he was always a stranger, ill at ease in a world beyond his comprehension. Given his background he of course had done exceptionally well in rising to the rank of major, then lieutenant colonel, in a supposedly elite service such as the Soviet Military Intelligence Service (GRU). At the time when he left the first envelope for the vice consul in Vienna he was young, could look forward to a long life, and hope for still further advancement. Moreover, as an intelligence officer he enjoyed considerably more freedom than most Russians, for he was a guardian of Soviet society, not one of the guarded. Yet freedom without a purpose, without a goal, can in itself be confusing, even unsettling. Though Popov longed to function as an individual, not simply as one cog in a system, he could not survive alone. As an alternative to returning passively to the Soviet fold he ultimately surrendered body and soul to the Americans.

Pyotr Popov was born in July 1923 in a financially distressed area near the northern reaches of the Volga River. The entire village was extremely poor; the only advantage the Popov family enjoyed was the use of slightly more land than others (some of which they actually owned). The elder Popovs were virtually illiterate, and young Pyotr probably would have followed the same unambitious pattern of his predecessors had it not been for a strong-willed elder brother, Aleksandr, who insisted that Pyotr continue in school beyond the first two grades. For most children in the countryside education ended at that point. Had it not been for this remarkable sibling Pyotr would probably have carried on much as his forebears had. Like most Russian peasants Pyotr's father and mother were traditionalists who, even after the atheistic Revolution, still treasured the icon that graced one corner of their hut as an ever-present symbol of God's will, and which seemed for the most part to function as a guarantee of a largely immutable world.

Pyotr himself, however, was born into a time of change that happened to coincide with a period of relative, albeit brief, good fortune for the Russian peasantry. Lenin had temporarily relaxed the centralized Communist economic system and had even allowed a return to both a money economy and certain types of private landholdings. The youngest of the Popovs thus came into the world in a momentary period of surcease from the imperious will of the Communist gods in Moscow, his childhood was a relatively happy one, and in later years he had nothing but pleasant memories of life with his family.

These and other facts emerged in informal meetings Popov held with George Kisevalter, a CIA representative who soon became more than just Popov's case officer; his role quickly evolved into that of a father or elder brother to Pyotr, and would remain so until near the end of Pyotr's short life. Kisevalter came from a highly educated family who lived in Russia during his youth; he was equally at home speaking Russian and English. The meetings of these two men were friendly affairs, though Popov's intelligence reporting always came first. After that, sitting in a safe house over drinks, Popov talked of whatever came to mind:

> I can remember as a boy on a small farm, we didn't have many material things such as fine clothing . . . but my mother managed to sew something together so that we were properly dressed.
>
> We never had any hired help. We did all our work with our own backs.
>
> . . . We barely had enough to eat, but . . . we had plenty of

potatoes. Everything was neat and clean at home . . . and it seemed as though we lived well.

As has already been suggested, the dominant figure in the family was Pyotr's elder brother, Aleksandr, of whom Pyotr spoke more often than of any other relative. Aleksandr was a physical giant, a man with little education but "a very decisive character." After their father died of cancer in 1929 it was Aleksandr who took responsibility for raising his younger brother.

Unfortunately for people like the Popovs, a basic change in the Russian peasantry's situation began in 1929 when Pyotr was six years old. Stalin had by then seized power after Lenin's death, and as he surveyed the agricultural situation of the Soviet Union he was not pleased. Finding that only 1.7 percent of peasant households had been collectivized while the rest remained private property, the dictator posed one of those famous Socratic questions that so frequently boded ill for his countrymen: "Can the Soviet system persist for long on these heterogeneous foundations?" he asked, immediately answering his own question with an angry "No!" Collectivization on a massive scale was launched soon thereafter, hitting particularly hard such people as the Popovs who were sole owners of some of the land they cultivated.

Pyotr spoke deprecatingly of the behavior of the so-called "poor peasants," people who did not own *any* of their own land and who were mobilized by the Moscow regime against those better off. Even before the Revolution the latter were sometimes regarded as *kulaks*.[3] In practice this vicious strategy of pitting the two economic classes against each other, though successful elsewhere, did not work in the Popovs' area. Many of the *kulaks* there were village leaders respected by the other inhabitants and frequently blood relatives of those poorer than themselves. The villagers therefore refused to be divided neatly into categories designated by the Party, insisting instead on maintaining a group solidarity that government emissaries sent to col-

lectivize the farms found frustrating and impenetrable. "I lived
through all that myself," Popov told Kisevalter, "and have seen what
they did; as a result of it, they created hatred throughout the entire
land." The injustice never ceased to rankle him.

> Take a simple peasant. . . . He would work from four in the morn-
> ing until ten at night and have enough of the basic food that con-
> stitutes a high standard of living for a peasant. He would have his
> black bread, some cucumbers, potatoes, and mushrooms. On holi-
> days he would have a piece of meat. He would even have a pair of
> shoes—leather ones, I mean. These would last him a lifetime. With
> these shoes he would come to church on Sundays. He walked bare-
> foot to the church, of course, then put on his shoes to enter. After
> church he would sling his shoes over his shoulder and again go
> barefoot back to his home.

These were the sort of people, Popov raged, whom the Communists
denigrated as *kulaks*. At Stalin's orders many of them "would be suddenly seized, and without trial shipped off to distant areas!"

Though the Popov family owned two horses and two or three
cows, and were thus prosperous by comparison with some of the others, they fortunately were not in the category of those well-to-do
enough to be subject to deportation. Their farm, however, was on the
list for collectivization. The first action against them, designed to
weaken their resistance, was the levy of a confiscatory five-fold
increase in their taxes. On this subject Popov exploded:

> We had to pay two thousand rubles, they said! Where would one
> get such a sum? It was physically impossible. We did not pay, so
> they came to our house to make a list of our property. I remember
> this as if it were yesterday. In our house there was the icon in the
> corner, a table here, an armchair there, a wardrobe, and a stove in
> the corner. The Communists came and listed every item. Then they

went to my brother, who was sitting in the armchair, and asked
him to sign the certificate, because he was the eldest male. A small
man, a party member, handed my brother the certificate. My
brother tore it up, seized this man and threw him straight at the
heavy wooden door. He hit the door so hard that it swung open,
and he flew out of the house.

After that episode terror spread throughout the village, and other
peasants came to consult Aleksandr. Following his advice they agreed
to write a joint letter to a hero of the Soviet revolution, Mikhail
Kalinin, who by then had become the country's president. This letter
was evidently written by some unusually educated person, since there
is reference to its having been in rhyme. The letter protested elo-
quently that the residents of the village were being unreasonably and
mercilessly abused, even being threatened with deportation. It pleaded for Kalinin's personal intervention.

The odds against such a plea being answered were enormous.
Even though Kalinin had been publicized by the Soviet government as
the "all-Russian peasant elder," he had heartily endorsed "*dekulak-
ization*," which he called "a kind of prophylactic measure, an anti-
capitalist vaccination." There were nevertheless rumblings of
discontent, even within the bureaucracy itself, over the harshness of
the anti-*kulak* program. Even people within the OGPU (a predecessor
of the KGB) had reported unfavorably on the process, alleging that
the slogan of those who so happily stripped wealth from others was
"Drink, eat—it's all ours!" The letter to Kalinin was answered by
orders, direct from Moscow, that canceled the deportations and in
particular ordered restitution of their property to the Popov family. A
commissar from a higher echelon of government arrived to see personally to the liberation of prospective deportees who had, meanwhile, been imprisoned.

As a result of this victory over bureaucracy Aleksandr was offered

a leadership position in the newly established local *kolkhoz,* or collective farm. But that was not for him. He turned down the offer and
at the same time requested governmental permission for himself,
along with his wife and children, to leave the *kolkhoz* entirely. He had
been a sergeant in the Soviet Army, he was a crack shot, and he
planned to support himself as a hunter. Since there was no way to col-
lectivize hunters in the wilderness, the government's assent was grudgingly given on condition that Aleksandr "buy" the release of his
family from the collective farm, which he was soon able to do.
Together they moved to a nearby territory belonging to the State
Lumber Trust, where Aleksandr built a log cabin, grew vegetables,
and, by poaching out of season, obtained venison. Against all odds
this remarkable man in effect became a private entrepreneur.

Aleksandr's experience is relevant to Pyotr's future as a spy,
because it is hard to see much difference in principle between
Aleksandr's hunting and his younger brother's spying. Both men
defied convention in order to earn their living through individual
enterprise. Aleksandr's stubbornness had two immediate consequences. Having established himself as a hunter, the elder brother
returned to the village to arrange for Pyotr to attend school in a nearby town. "One of us Popovs should be educated," he pronounced.
Educational standards were not high in the countryside, and even
instruction in the Russian language was mediocre. Yet under the stratified system of the vaunted "classless society" the literate formed a
virtual caste apart.[4]

The second consequence of Aleksandr's feat was less pleasant.
Every blessing, Aleksandr warned, carries with it some penalty, which
in this case meant that Pyotr had to learn to wear leather shoes to
school every day instead of just on Sundays (a painful experience for
one who was used to wearing only felt boots or, in warm weather,
lapti, the peasant footwear woven from reeds). Going to school
beyond the second grade, however, was so unusual that it involved a

major transition in the life of the young man. Along with the awesome
aura of advancing further in the social scale than any of Pyotr's peers
had imagined, there came a compulsory modification of both behavior and dress. He gritted his teeth, carried the shoes with him every
morning, and put them on just before entering the school building.
Before the long walk home, of course, he switched back to something
more comfortable.

By the early 1930s other reforms had been made in the Soviet educational system that returned it in structure, if not in subject matter,
to the pre-Revolutionary system. The emphasis was on somehow
refashioning an entire generation by eliminating illiteracy, though
standards were not high and even the history of the Soviet civil war
was frequently neglected. Conformity was the highest goal. Students
who had become members of the national Communist youth organization and displayed their willingness to follow Party policy fared better than others, and we know that at some point Popov did formally
become a Communist. If during these years he was following the pattern that characterized him later, he must surely have been giving the
impression of being a dutiful citizen without in fact having any real
sense of obligation to the Soviet state.

When it came to conformity, the all-important key to survival,
Pyotr excelled while many others did not. He attended classes, for
example, with unruly "semi-orphans" who had lost one or sometimes
both of their parents as a result of the regime's increasingly repressive
measures that had culminated in massive arrests and deportations to
Siberia. Not only were the schools expected to conquer illiteracy, their
duty was to tame the *beznadzornye* (unsupervised ones), many of
whom presented severe disciplinary problems. Meanwhile the good
boy, Pyotr, conformed outwardly then as he did later, and his conformity was understandably (though mistakenly) accepted by teachers
and other authorities as political commitment.

MILITARY CAREER

In the troubled years that followed, while the threat from Nazi Germany became increasingly ominous, nationwide education was accelerated; like many others of his generation Pyotr, considered a good student, was hastily granted a school certificate and sent off to join the Red Army. Once in its ranks his education, slight though it was, qualified him for officer training, and he graduated in 1942 with the temporary rank of junior lieutenant. This was no great achievement: war had been raging for three years and lieutenants were a form of cannon fodder greatly in demand.

Though wounded in active combat, Popov had remarkably few war stories to tell his CIA case officer in Vienna. As he related his experiences under interrogation his life was not without dramatic potential, yet he lacked the power to evoke it. War was a phenomenon too immense for him to comprehend, even though he had been personally involved. Take, for example, the battle in and around Tula, a city located south of Moscow. Not yet commissioned, Popov had been in training there when he and his fellow cadets found themselves in the path of Gen. Heinz Guderian, the George Patton of Nazi Germany, whose Second Tank Army launched the final German effort to capture the capital in November–December 1941.[5] The battle at Tula was a turning point in the war because the Nazi forces were stopped cold. Yet during interrogations Popov never dwelt on this struggle. Many were killed and the city was demolished by air strikes, but to judge from his own words Popov carried out his duties almost distractedly, a sort of eternal bystander. He never bragged of his prowess, never complained of or lauded his commanders, never displayed more than mild antipathy toward the Germans and Austrians who had been Russia's enemies.

It was obvious that he scarcely distinguished the effects of war from those that followed the advent of peace. As a peasant from a distant corner of Russia, to whom any voice from far-off Moscow carried a threat rather than a promise, he had no reason to identify with his nation. Had he been brought up in a city he would have beheld ceremonies, sporting events, festivities even, to celebrate solidarity among Russians. But patriotism had no significance within the narrow focus of his life. The icon situated in the corner of his family's home may at one time have carried a hint of higher values, but as he grew up such abstractions meant less and less to him.

Only with the Red Army itself did Popov develop a limited bond, as illustrated by his unfavorable comparison of the fighting qualities of Western armies with those of the Soviets. At the time of his defection, however, that connection could only have been a superficial prejudice, for he had never personally witnessed a Western army in action. Indeed, he knew surprisingly little about military matters in general, and the fact that he became an officer at all seems to have been more a matter of chance than choice. Throughout his life Popov had simply taken advantage of opportunities that unexpectedly presented themselves, and his rise to the rank of lieutenant colonel did not appear to have anything to do with either patriotism or military skill.

Look for a moment at Popov's advancement in one of the crucial periods of the war. In late 1944, wounded and hospitalized, he was interviewed by a board of officers seeking candidates for three years of advanced training at the Frunze Military Academy in Moscow. Such an achievement was a great honor, but what were Pyotr's qualifications? By this time he had been twice promoted, reaching the rank of senior lieutenant, and was on the verge of being raised to captain. Even more fortunately for him, his peasant background was now considered an asset guaranteeing true proletarian sympathies, and sketchy military records carried no reference to his family's having once been classified as *kulaks*. In addition he met the generally stringent formal qualifications for membership in the Communist party, and did not hesitate to join it, despite his total lack of ideological commitment. Given the enormous casualty rate during the war, the Red Army was scraping hard to find career officers and, on paper at least, Popov more than fulfilled the minimum requirements of the academy, not the least of which was simply being alive and physically fit. Indeed, the war had already taken such a toll that only 90 candidates could be recruited for his class (against a quota of 150).

In connection with his assignment to Frunze, Popov had one request to make. Somewhere along the line he had met and married Galina Petrovna, a quiet young woman who taught German in an elementary school in Kalinin. He asked for living quarters in Moscow that they could occupy while he was a student, and his request was granted. The pair had but one room to themselves, and had to share a kitchen and bath with four other families. But this one room was home.

Luck always played a considerable role in Popov's career. The key event that eventually made him useful to the Americans was being sent on to another advanced school—euphemistically known as the Military-Diplomatic Academy—after graduating from Frunze. The intentionally misleading name for the academy had nothing whatsoever to do with diplomacy, but rather was the training establishment for Soviet military intelligence officers who were intended to function, more aggressively than their counterparts in the U.S. Army, by personally engaging in subversion and the recruitment of spies.

Upon graduation this naive and likable but not at all forceful man was sent abroad to a totally alien environment, with the mission of collecting "strategic intelligence" on behalf of his country. A more unlikely person could not have been chosen for the task. ("Strategic intelligence" is the data and evaluative procedures that go into forming the major military and political decisions of world powers.) From his subsequent performance it was obvious to his American associates that Popov had not been able to grasp even the basic terminology of routine military intelligence, much less the recondite procedures necessary to recruit spies who would give him access to other nations' most cherished secrets. Yet the latter was the very task to which he was now expected to address himself.

MILITARY INTELLIGENCE ASSIGNMENT — VIENNA

Military intelligence sometimes involves work that could be performed by a skillfully computerized robot, but Popov was not assigned to any such undemanding tasks. Instead in 1951 he was sent to Vienna, a highly sophisticated city of 1.5 million people whose language, culture, and history were totally unknown to him. Though it was his first experience in the non-Russian world, there is little record of Popov's early reaction to it. Inherently apolitical yet trying hard to seem a man of the world, he appears to have reacted by merely avoiding the discussion of subjects such as politics, of which he had little understanding.[6] His adjustment to a charming city of palaces and parks was influenced by the fact that most Soviet military forces, once finding themselves abroad, usually tried to shield their personnel from both culture shock and venal temptations; they believed that to do otherwise would cause their fighting men to degenerate into a self-indulgent rabble. The Soviet Army was even more solicitous than the Americans in trying to protect their officers and men, not just from boredom but from the much more dangerous problems of sedition and corruption. Discipline was strict, hours were long, and the work-week lasted six days, ending at eight P.M. on Saturdays. Sundays were meant to be filled with participation in group sports or cultural outings, whereas the pursuit of individual interests was strongly—though not always effectively—discouraged. To this regimentation Popov reacted as he had to other such challenges: outward conformity but inward revolt.

With no choice but superficial conventionality, Popov lived with his wife in the Grand Hotel, one of Vienna's finest, and made token appearances at the GRU office located not far away at another hotel, the Imperial. Full of glitter and glamour, both establishments had until

1945 been the haunts of Nazi officers who, under the crystal chande-
liers, flaunted their superiority during much of Austria's seven-year
union with Hitler's Reich. Neither the beauty nor the drama of this
setting, however, seems to have made any impression on Popov—
none, at least, that he could put into words.

Popov was of course expected to take his meals seven days a week
at the military mess in the Grand, and was also constrained (much
against his will) to participate in organized recreation; his absence,
unless he gave advance notice along with some official justification,
would be unfavorably noted. At the beginning he appears to have conformed, using much of his spare time to play billiards, table tennis,
and basketball with his cohorts. But such pastimes were really not for
him. Having no knack for conviviality, he was ill at ease with his fellow officers and possibly handicapped by being the only one among
them who came from a peasant background. It was therefore fortunate that intelligence collection is an occupation peculiarly suited to
those with a solitary bent; the recruitment of spies cannot be carried
out in platoon formation with bayonets fixed. Popov thus happily
took advantage of his intelligence "operations," fictitious though they
often were, as ideal excuses for absence from organized recreation.

At least in his early days in Vienna, Popov's "operations" were
pretexts, and no more. Ideally he should have been able to blend into
the Viennese community in his search for persons willing and able to
spy on the Allies. With no schooling in the German language this task
was far beyond his imagination and capabilities. Nonetheless, neither
in Austria nor in Moscow did Popov's failings go unnoticed. He was
criticized by his superior in Vienna, Colonel Yegorov, and even more
severely admonished when, called to Moscow in April 1954, he
reported to GRU Headquarters. Popov was told bluntly, as he later
admitted to the ever-sympathetic Kisevalter, that "my recruiting
efforts have brought in insignificant results. You can read more material in the newspapers than these agents bring in, they say."

Popov Prefers American Employment

At the root of Popov's preference for the Americans over the Soviets was the simple fact that his CIA contacts made clear that they valued him not just as an agent but as a friend. He appears literally never to have had a close acquaintance and confidant—he had never been able to bare his feelings, not even to his wife, now with him in Vienna. Yet he somehow could do so with Kisevalter. For the first time in Pyotr's troubled life someone obviously superior in rank and education was treating him not just as an equal but also as a valued human being.

By contrast, his dealings with his Soviet superiors were rigidly formal. It was the fashion in the Red Army to rap out orders quickly and curtly, in a manner that implied disdain. The insinuation of contempt may indeed have been more than a mere product of the military mores; the army was the opposite of a classless society and Popov was clearly regarded by his superiors as a peasant. He himself was well aware of their prejudices.

Popov's relations with his new American employers, on the other hand, unfolded as easily as if he had just quietly moved in to stay with relatives. He felt so little need to rationalize his clandestine defection that it was a long time before he was even half able to articulate his reasons. Though for many men in his position defection was a major, life-changing trauma, in his case it seems instead to have been a surcease from intolerable strain. No wonder, really, for it is not apparent that he had any sense of patriotism or even fondness for his country. I cannot help but contrast him with the Russian exiles I remember while living abroad in my youth. They were well educated and multilingual, as at ease in the languages of Western Europe as in their own, and also had in common the fact of having fled Russia to save their lives. Most of them were titled, though uniformly impoverished, and reduced to being nursemaids or tutors. Yet they would regale me, for as long as a child's attention span permitted, with tales of their homeland. Despite the horrors of the Revolution they still loved Mother Russia. For Popov, on the other hand, the concept of a motherland as an object of love and obedience did not exist. His defection was in no way ideological.

MOTIVATION

Let us review what we learned about him through his relationship with the CIA to try to fathom what motivated him to collaborate. In his first clandestine meeting with CIA representatives Popov disclosed, almost incidentally, that he was offering his services because he "had an affair to straighten out." The "affair" was not one of principle or politics; instead it centered quite simply on how to support two women simultaneously. As he explained, he had no better ideas of his own: "As an extreme measure, I finally decided to come to you." To ask for money, of course, in return for information on the Soviet Army, it goes without saying. What else did he have to sell?

It turned out that before he passed his note to the vice consul, Popov had already made several similar approaches. In connection with those previous attempts, however, he had refused to reveal his identity or organizational affiliation, and therefore was rejected. Utterly naive as an intelligence officer, he had forgotten (if he ever knew it) the first criterion of his profession: intelligence is only as good as the source from which it comes. Thus the attempt to keep his identity secret was fruitless; Vienna was too full of con artists trying to pass as potential spies for any such disingenuous appeal to work. Only after he had displayed his Soviet identity card—and, even then, with his name cautiously blocked out by his thumb—did the barriers begin to crumble. This man was worth at least the time required for an interrogation, precisely because he *was* so cautious. By contrast, intelligence fabricators were always willing to brandish their spurious qualifications; since Popov did not, there was reason to think he was genuine.

Once his bona fides had been accepted and an agreement had been reached on the terms of future collaboration, Popov was advanced a relatively modest sum of money in Austrian schillings. After punctiliously expressing his gratitude, he followed up with a request that was almost a prayer: "The only thing is," he pleaded, "treat me like a human being!" That unexpected utterance shed considerable light on his defection. Popov was not only seeking money, he wanted a sense of real worth. Such reassurance, unattainable from his harsh Soviet superiors, was what the Americans henceforth gave him.

Though it appeared from the outset that his Soviet superiors considered Popov's performance substandard, he was effective as a CIA agent. The difference lay in the fact that, contrary to the Soviets, his American associates could impose requirements on him that were well within his capabilities. The Russians wanted information on decision-making processes taking place within the three Vienna headquarters of the western Allies—Great Britain, France, and the United States. Popov had no access to those organizations, nor could he speak any of their languages. He could not have struck up even the most casual of conversations with an American, British, or French officer even had they happened to meet in some public place. By contrast, what the CIA representatives asked of him was information, preferably in documentary form, from the Soviet headquarters in Vienna out of which Popov worked. Having by then been promoted to lieutenant colonel, he could move largely unchallenged wherever he wished within that headquarters and, though there were some limitations on the documents he could see, the majority were freely available to him. A considerable number of those documents were directly relevant to the subject uppermost in the minds of the Western leaders and their peoples: the possibility of war with Russia.

Consider for a moment the political situation of the time. Stalin appeared progressively paranoid and his mental instability was causing widespread alarm throughout the West. An invasion by

Communist forces such as those that had overwhelmed South Korea in 1950 was, in theory, equally possible in Austria. If such a Soviet takeover were to occur, would the newly established North Atlantic Treaty Organization (NATO) risk war to defend Austria, one of the smallest countries in Europe? Uncertainty prevailed. The Korean War was not necessarily relevant as a precedent, for though each side had inflicted terrible punishment on the other, the Asian conflict ended without a retributive victory over the northern aggressor. Nonetheless, the fear of another sneak attack, this time taking place in the West, was the bugaboo of American intelligence in Europe in the early years after World War II. The situation in turn made penetration of the GRU a high priority.

Intelligence organizations arc valued as targets in themselves, simply because their files are repositories of critically important information. But equally important is the way such organizations are themselves configured—the number of people they devote selectively to certain tasks instead of others, the degree of emphasis on other countries' order of battle (troop strength and distribution of func tions), the amount of effort devoted to subversion—all these details, and many others like them, reveal a great deal about an army's military focus and intentions. In sum, the intelligence service of a military force intent on aggression will seek different types of information than one whose mission is purely defensive.

When Popov obtained a complete organization chart of the GRU in Austria, together with names and particulars about the officers in charge of various functions—as he did early on for the CIA—his work counted as a major achievement. The GRU's structure, as revealed by the chart, gave no indication of aggressive intent on the part of the Russians, and was therefore highly valued by the headquarters of the Western Allies. It was a great feather in Popov's cap in the eyes of those few in the CIA who knew about his acquisition.

Poor Performance for the GRU

While Popov's performance was eminently satisfactory to his American friends, what he produced on behalf of his Soviet superiors continued to be below par. Faced with his poor performance against the three Allied headquarters in Vienna, his GRU superiors redirected his efforts toward the Eastern European refugee community, an easy to mine yet fairly fecund field since the Russians were always mindful of the subversive threat posed by Soviet Bloc refugees beyond their official control. Thousands of such fugitives and exiles had found shelter in Vienna, mainly nationals of countries that had fallen into Communist hands as the Soviet Army drove back the Germans— Yugoslavs, Czechs, Bulgarians, and others—who feared Communist domination as much as they had feared the Nazis. Once under the protective mantle of the West they felt relatively secure, though always edgy because of unrelenting Soviet hostility.

At a minimum Popov's training should have prepared him for the task of recruiting agents within this exile community. While the majority of the "displaced persons" (as the Allied governments officially labeled them) were anti-Communist, most were very poor as well. Working secretly for a Soviet intelligence officer was at least one way to eke out a living, regardless of how objectionable it was to them politically. Yet even such readily available prey was beyond Popov's reach. Making what in American intelligence jargon is called a "cold pitch" by asking a person he didn't know to spy for him was something Popov simply could not bring himself to do; whether such behavior violated his sense of decency or whether he could not bear the threat of rejection, we shall never know. Whatever the reason, he was no more able to recruit a spy than he could have walked naked through the center of Vienna.

Faced with this impasse, Milica Kohanek, a Serbian woman who became Popov's mistress, was made to order for him in every way.

When he confessed his own shortcomings to her, she was ready to help. No ideological questions divided them; as a member of the Austrian Communist Party she considered members of Vienna's largely anti-Communist Yugoslav community fair game and suffered from none of the embarrassing shyness that inhibited her lover. What could be learned through modest penetrations of refugee organizations was, of course, a far cry from the "strategic intelligence" Popov had originally been dispatched to Vienna to collect, but no matter! Many intelligence officers—Americans included—have learned that turning in some paper, *any* paper, to their superiors is better for their careers than turning in none.

As to satisfying his own pride, Popov obviously felt fulfilled as a result of what he collected for the GRU through "Mili," most of it on the subject of refugee political activity in Vienna. Moreover, Mili soon became more than just a helpmate; Popov was clearly in love with her, even though she was no beauty. A member of the CIA station who observed the couple in a restaurant wrote that she "must, in truth, have hidden charms since it is open to question that even her mother could love her face." To Popov, however, she provided a welcome surcease from the regimented life of the Grand Hotel. Since his conduct was a violation of regulations, the time spent with her was ascribed to "intelligence collection"; he was certainly not the first case officer, regardless of nationality, to take such liberties. In any case he and Milica enjoyed outings in the Prater or along the Danube, and attended public events such as boxing matches. Popov even bought two bicycles, which he kept at her house, plus a small boat for their use on the river—both purchases made possible by money earned from the CIA. Yet, despite all the time he spent with Mili he was never demonstrative in his affection; from listening to him one might have thought their relationship was a largely professional one. He did, however, like to emphasize her docility, assuring Kisevalter that she would cause no trouble vis-à-vis his family.

"She is a sensible girl," he said. "She knows I have a wife and children. . . . But, she's used to me now. In general I have a plain Russian soul; if she is lacking anything I will give her all I have, *whether I have it or not.*[7] But she cannot in any way have a claim on me." What constitutes a claim is, of course, always a matter of definition, but Popov's extramarital relationship was at least sufficiently stable for Milica to become pregnant by him three times. She then had three abortions at his—and, indirectly, the CIA's—expense. What her feelings toward Popov truly were will never be known, but it seems likely she was not as docile as he pretended. When the Soviet Army invaded Hungary, for example, she became openly disenchanted with the Austrian Communist Party and created great commotion by exposing the Party's stuffing of ballot boxes in an Austrian election. Eventually she renounced Communism completely. Her relationship with Popov, however, continued unabated until near the end of his life and was eventually to have serious consequences for him.

GROWING LOYALTY TO THE UNITED STATES

The longer Popov worked for the CIA the more his loyalty shifted completely to the United States. One of the high points of his career was the receipt of a present from then-director of Central Intelligence, Allen Dulles. The CIA chief of station met with Popov to present a gift of specially made gold cuff links. They symbolized, Popov was told, the strong link between the Soviet lieutenant colonel and his American friends—though, as they explained it, for security reasons "the design is of an entirely innocuous nature. Its symbolism comes from Greek mythology. The helmet of Athena denotes wisdom, and the sword denotes bravery. . . . It has no American tone." What Popov made of such statements we have no way of knowing; never having heard of Athena he was probably totally bewildered.

Nonetheless, the chief clearly made the point that the cuff links also had a practical use as a recognition device; an identical pair were held at CIA headquarters, to be used in establishing the bona fides of any emissary who might be sent to contact Popov later, either in the Soviet Union or in some other place. Popov was grateful. Contrasting the treatment he received from the Americans with that accorded him by the GRU, he said of the latter organization, "They are never concerned about how dangerous an assignment may be. They are only interested in squeezing all they can out of a person." And later, "You [Americans] find time to drink and relax. It is an entirely human approach. You have respect for an individual. . . . With us, of course, the individual is nothing, and the government interest is everything."

Yet by 1955 when his stay in Austria was drawing to an end, even under gentle and friendly American tutelage Popov was showing the strain of his double life, as manifested by continuing headaches and high blood pressure. He was considerably buoyed, nonetheless, when he received a commendation from Soviet higher headquarters and learned that he had been recommended for promotion to full colonel. For that Popov gave a major share of the credit to his mistress, who had produced a great deal of the intelligence on refugee activity that he then handed on to the GRU. "My girl, Mili, was a big help to me," he said, with masterly understatement.

The attachment to Milica had indeed become stronger than ever, and he could not face squarely the idea of leaving her. Talking about their separation as if it were she who had all the regrets, he would say, "My girl is very sad. She knows I have not promised her anything, but she is accustomed to me." Then he would talk, unrealistically (given her break with the Austrian Communists), of her coming to Moscow as a delegate to a Democratic Youth Congress. "I will take care of her while she is in Moscow. And if possible, will keep her there, find her work." Milica, of course, would never have dared visit the Soviet Union or any other Communist land following her break with the Austrian Party. Yet she was to remain in Popov's thoughts and definitively influence his life until the end.

Popov's wife and children are scarcely mentioned in his meetings with his CIA case officers. They joined him in Vienna after his relationship with Mili, which had begun partly out of loneliness, was already well established. Despite his affair Popov had a strong sense of family loyalty and was concerned that no harm come to his wife and children.

In Popov's dislike of his country, as it had been since the Revolution, he was in fact typical of many of his compatriots who had at one time or another lived abroad. A study based on a sample of 320 personal history statements and interviews with Russian émigrés in the early post–World War II period showed that 83 percent of them gave "exposure to the West" as the reason for their expatriation. By contrast, only 6 percent cited "no freedom," and 2 percent mentioned "standard of living." It is clear, therefore, that it was the *overall* Russian situation that repelled them, not just one or more of its particular shortcomings.

Popov, after returning to Vienna from an official visit to GRU headquarters in Moscow in mid-1955, was even more discouraged than usual.

> It is terrible to see how people live in our villages. . . . In Kalinin, the province center only one hundred kilometers from Moscow, butter cannot be bought; sugar can be had on rare occasions. . . . People come to Moscow from Kostroma, which means a twelve-hour train ride, just to buy food. Other cities don't have a damn thing. . . . From my village, some people went to Gorky to buy food, but there was nothing there.

Talking about the village where he had grown up, Popov said:

> Every time I come home hundreds of people, in fact all of them, are without bread. And they turn to me and say, "You have come from the city; please tell us, when will we be able to live as human

beings?" What can I say? What? As a Communist Party man I tell
them that until they begin to work properly and restore order in
the *kolkhoz*, they will have no bread. At the same time, I know
myself this is all nonsense.

Popov was not alone in his resentment. Others were in fact less
cautious than he. "Among the complement of officers who have been
abroad," he said, "there is constant expression of dissatisfaction with
respect to our regime. I recently heard one officer say, 'Just look at
that unemployed Austrian's apartment. It is much better than my
quarters as an officer in Moscow!'" Most of Popov's colleagues in
Vienna were more sophisticated than he, yet their feelings about their
homeland were not dissimilar to his. One of them, reflecting on the
climate of unrest within Russia itself, commented:

> It seems as though a certain stream of daring has been poured into
> this group of people [the Soviet officer corps in Vienna]. . . . This
> has been true historically. In the course of the war of 1812–1814,
> tsarist Russian officers went as far as Paris, and from there they
> brought back new ideas which gave impetus to land reform and
> the liberation of the serfs.

Leaving the past behind, Popov then took up where the other officer had left off.

> Today a similar stream of influence is felt among the officer com-
> plement. Of course, the officer corps is a privileged group. We are
> far more fortunate than others in the USSR, though each individual
> is afraid to speak out for fear of losing his advantages. Today there
> is very little patriotism as such.

On several occasions Popov also quoted another colleague, a lieutenant colonel who was given to such inflammatory statements as "I
consider it an absolute error to have abolished private property. This
has removed the last vestige of individual initiative from the

peasants." Popov claimed he was always careful to make no rejoinder for fear that his colleague might be acting as a provocateur. For Popov's part, however, he did not believe in the possibility of a revolution against the Communists. "I doubt whether any overt, antigovernment movement or action could take place. . . . There is absolutely no way for the peasants to organize. There is no leadership. There is no opposition. There are many who have hopes for a change, but those are only hopes."

Perhaps recalling the advice that his brother Aleksandr had given him many years before "to milk the system for everything he could get," Popov described the attitude of Soviet officialdom:

> If anyone in the USSR is placed in some government job that permits him to chisel some benefit for himself, he certainly does it. It makes no difference what the position is; it can even be that of a minister. . . . The salt of the matter is this: since there is such abject poverty and he is hungry, of necessity he is forced to think first of his own welfare.

TRANSFER TO EAST GERMANY

In 1955 the Allied occupation of Austria ended and the country was restored to independence as a neutral state. With this neutralization Soviet forces began a rapid pull-out and Popov, like most other officers, had little idea what the future held. Suddenly he was gone, transferred first back to Moscow and shortly thereafter to the city of Schwerin, deep in the Soviet Zone of Germany and completely out of touch with his CIA friends.

After unsuccessful attempts to reestablish contact with the Americans, Popov took advantage of an opportunity that presented itself one evening in January 1956. He had noticed a British mission car parked outside a Baltic Sea resort hotel and took the bold step of locating the owner's room and knocking on the door to ask for help. He introduced himself as a Soviet lieutenant colonel working at the

intelligence headquarters in Schwerin who had been trying unsuccessfully to make contact with American officers. He explained that he
had come without the knowledge of his chief.

Popov recounted his life history to the British officer, beginning
with his miserable days on the farm, and then went on to talk about
his relationship with the Americans. He had tried to recontact them,
he said, via "a reliable lady named Mili," but without success. He
therefore wanted the British officer's help in reestablishing contact
with the Americans so that he could send them "a most important top
secret directive of the Central Committee of the Communist Party of
the USSR." At that point he produced a diary, which he alleged contained a transcript from a secret Soviet Army pamphlet concerning the
use of atomic weapons, and asked the British officer to send it, together with a letter, to American authorities.

Once the Americans learned from the British of this encounter,
efforts were immediately made to reestablish communications with
Popov. Two members—"A" and "B"—of the United States Military
Liaison Mission were carefully selected for the job. B spoke Russian.
Having regularly visited points in East Germany in the past, the two
were expected to recontact Popov, acknowledge his message, and
establish a communication channel. Makeshift arrangements had fortunately already been set up, with considerable presence of mind, by
the British officer whom Popov had contacted out of the blue.

Russian-speaking B was to be the main player in this risky but
rather comic episode. Arriving at a café in the resort previously selected jointly by Popov and the British officer, the two Americans prepared to meet Popov in the men's toilet at 9:10 P.M. After settling in
at a table, B ordered a drink for a notional stomach disorder. At the
appointed hour he went to the men's room and waited. When an East
German soldier entered several minutes later the captain pretended to
be ill and vomited. He waited an additional several minutes and, since
no one came, he left.

Meanwhile Popov appears to have arrived at the café but he and the non-Russian speaking A had made no attempt at contact. It was B who took the initiative as soon as he emerged from the men's room. Recognition must have stemmed from B's having seen a photograph of Popov, while the guileless Popov might have been prepared to confide in just about anyone wearing a U.S. officer's uniform. At that point the charade became repetitive. B again repaired to the men's room, expecting Popov to follow him there. Popov did not follow, possibly because he had no instructions to do so or, alternatively, due to some compunction about using a toilet as a meeting place. (In his native language he might have described such a contact as *nekulturniy*, uncultured.) B therefore waited fruitlessly, another stranger walked in, and the captain once again, to explain his extended presence in the toilet, pretended to vomit. In any case this procedure was repeated twice more, without Popov joining B.

Finally A came to the toilet to tell B that Popov, after an hour, had left the café. The two Americans decided to return to their hotel rooms. Having taken the stairs, upon reaching the second floor they ran into Popov. He had been accosted by two drunken Germans, but the approach of the Americans apparently distracted them, allowing Popov time to slip away to the hall toilet. There he was quickly accosted by B. After the two men had established each other's identities, Popov passed a red-covered notebook containing fifty-eight pages of intelligence reports plus four pages of instructions regarding future meetings.

Since Popov was stationed in an area of East Germany where it would be difficult for an American to contact him, arrangements were made for an elderly German from West Berlin to serve as courier. The old man's bona fides would be established by his wearing duplicates of the cuff links presented to Popov in Vienna. Such courier runs carried out by the German were so carefully planned that Popov soon lost any apprehension he may originally have had. During a late April contact the courier noticed that Popov hummed throughout the meeting; when the courier commented on his good cheer Popov replied that "on some days he felt cheerful, and other days not so much so; but that this was one of his good days."

TRAVEL TO WEST BERLIN

In August of that year the courier, upon returning from East Germany, brought good news. Popov had sent word that, in connection with operational trips to Communist East Berlin, he would now be able to get to West Berlin. By October face-to-face meetings were already under way when Popov brought even better news. Working through two friends, both colonels like himself, he had arranged an intelligence assignment to Communist East Berlin. Once he arrived, in June 1957, he resumed his American contacts.

The Popov whom a CIA case officer met in West Berlin was, superficially at least, a more self-confident and worldly man than he had been at his initial contact in Vienna four and a half years earlier. No wonder, for what the Russians in East Germany had asked him to do was undemanding in the extreme. To recruit Germans to serve as Soviet agents it was only necessary to apply to either the East German police or the Communist Party, who would then come up with a list of appropriate candidates. The latter were, of course, unlikely to resist, so to fail at a such task was virtually impossible. Yet the GRU regularly handed out commendations for success. Popov himself was thus the beneficiary of the instinctual bureaucratic propensity for self-congratulation, a phenomenon perhaps even more pervasive in authoritarian countries than in democratic ones—most likely a heady experience, after years of disdain from his superiors.

Nonetheless, when he discussed at length the operations he was conducting from East Berlin on behalf of the GRU, Popov's CIA case officers noted that he seemed as indecisive and inefficient as ever. First among his problems was amazingly poor recall. Almost comical had it not been so potentially disastrous in an area such as Communist East Berlin, Popov had developed a propensity for forgetting the details of meeting plans. He arrived in West Berlin for his second encounter with a CIA man there, but was unable to recall the location of the safe house. To make matters worse he had left behind a notebook containing emergency telephone numbers—a mnemonic device especially prepared for him by one of his American handlers. He returned to East Berlin and made a long-distance call to his wife in Schwerin to get the necessary CIA numbers and—with staggering disregard for security—actually made the call from the Soviet headquarters itself!

The efficiency of meeting arrangements was slow to improve, even though the CIA installed a red-lettered nameplate on the door of the West Berlin safe apartment to ensure that their agent did not by error enter the wrong dwelling. To make matters worse, by the fifth meeting since his move south from Schwerin, Popov had still not mastered the use of the Berlin public transportation system. On one dreadful occasion he took a rush hour S-Bahn express by mistake and was thereby carried nonstop from East Berlin through West Berlin to Potsdam. Once there he was immediately accosted by a Soviet military policeman. When Popov, who was in civilian clothes, showed his official military identity card, the MP insisted on calling the senior sergeant on duty. Once the problem was explained, the sergeant permitted Popov to board the S-Bahn back through West Berlin, but reported the incident through military channels. Popov was later reprimanded by his Soviet superior for having transited West Berlin without authorization. Furthermore, as late as October 1957 one of the agency case officers who met him in West Berlin noted that Popov forgot names as easily as he forgot instructions regarding specific information requests levied on him.

In addition to his memory problems, once in East Berlin Popov continued to alternate between unrealistic self-confidence and periods of despondency, the latter accompanied by recurrent headaches and high blood pressure. His moods quite often fluctuated within the span of a single meeting. For example, in August 1957, two months after being assigned to East Berlin, he said in reference to his GRU job: "In general, the work is not difficult here. During the past month I have already grasped our operations, and now I am capable of carrying out any assignment." Yet before the conversation ended his tone had changed completely and he became so nearly incoherent that the two case officers meeting with him feared he might break into tears as he said, "I certainly wish you would help me because otherwise things will not go well for me." Popov's voice trembled. "I don't mean really badly, but I do not wish to appear worse than the others!" Above all, he tried to explain, it was the double life he led that imposed so much stress on him.

> Maintaining contact with you is so nerve-racking, and on top of
> this there is great pressure to do my own work. All in addition to
> my Party job! In Party work, the Secretary should be the leader.
> This puts my head in a whirl.

TROUBLE AHEAD

Two months after this conversation the GRU gave Popov a task that later came back to haunt him. In October 1957 he was assigned to assist in dispatching a female Soviet agent named Tairova through Tempelhof Airport in Berlin. The case was ridiculous, in retrospect appearing to be a hopelessly miswritten novel.

Tairova, after training as a manicurist in Poland, England, and Paris, was to join her dipsomaniacal husband, who had already been in place in Brooklyn, New York, for three years. In intelligence jargon both were known as "illegals" (which is applied to a person who has not only been intensively trained in espionage but has also developed an elaborately documented false identity, usually as a citizen of some other country than his or her own). Popov saw Tairova off from the airport without incident, but the operation went awry soon after she arrived in the United States. In mid-1958, over a seemingly minor incident (centering on the fact that she shared an apartment with her husband before acquiring U.S. documentation to prove she was his wife), the couple was interrogated by the U.S. Immigration and Naturalization Service. For no other reason than the instinctive Russian fear of anyone who acts like a policeman, the couple panicked and returned to Moscow. To justify their action the duo claimed she had been under heavy hostile surveillance beginning at Tempelhof, and further alleged that the surveillance had continued in the United States. Although the claim concerning Tempelhof was false, Popov feared it would be taken seriously by the GRU and be considered a black mark against him by his own superiors in Berlin since he had been involved in sending her on her way. Popov was badly shaken by the incident, particularly when a GRU colonel arrived from Moscow to investigate the circumstances surrounding the debacle. "The colonel spoke to me yesterday," Popov told his case officer, "and I didn't sleep all night. . . . True, they have no evidence, but you see the chiefs in Moscow will never permit a suggestion that any of them could possibly have made an error. Somebody has to be guilty!" His tale ended on a note of despair. "So, you see, perhaps we shall never meet again!"

The "unpleasantness" concerning the illegals came at a bad time for Popov. In April he had been warned by his GRU superiors concerning his lack of accomplishment. He told his CIA case officer then: "Leonid Ivanovich [his GRU chief] scolds me. 'By the end of May I want two recruitments from you. . . . You run all over the place with people, but I don't see any results. Look at what your colleagues are doing!'" Faced with such criticism it is doubtful that Popov was able to present any coherent rebuttal, for his sense of inadequacy seemed to increase from week to week. Furthermore, soon after the debacle with the illegals, a semiannual review of his operations was scheduled and he had little to present in the way of accomplishment.

The final blow was nonetheless unexpectedly sudden. On 5 November 1958 Popov signaled for an urgent meeting with his case officer that very night. By the time he arrived at the safe house he was weeping and muttering incoherently because of still another problem. "Probably it's all over. . . . I'll be sent back . . . it's all because of Mili." As he took a seat he dried his eyes. "Excuse me for behaving this way."

An incident had occurred in late October that had brought Popov's continued relations with Milica to the attention of GRU Headquarters. By an unhappy coincidence, the particular GRU directorate in Moscow to which Popov was ultimately responsible was under fire from the Communist Party Central Committee for "lack of accomplishment," the same failing of which Popov himself had so often been accused, and the local GRU chief was therefore doubly motivated to record a success.

At first, on orders from Moscow, Popov was questioned about Mili; the GRU suspected that she must be "working for someone" since there was evidence that by 1957 she had become an informant for the Austrian police. This, together with the fact that she had broken with the Austrian Communist Party after having publicly exposed its involvement in an election fraud, magnified her continued relations with Popov into a security problem. Even in these difficult circumstances, however, Popov's resilient ability to face adversity was not long in asserting itself. Although forced to write a self-criticism of his relationship with Mili, he tried to make light of the affair. Predictably, he was not successful, and was therefore ordered to return to Moscow for further questioning, albeit under the guise of "operational discussions."

At this point the CIA was at fault in not going all out to dissuade him from complying. The most elementary knowledge of Soviet procedures in such cases clearly suggested that he should defect and be immediately evacuated to a safe haven. Instead, the agency let itself be influenced by Popov, whose bad judgment was by now legendary. He had lapsed suddenly into one of his irrationally optimistic phases and maintained, even though aware that he was in serious trouble over the Mili affair, that he could successfully rebut any and all charges with his memorable aphorism: "Should they tell me that I made a bad mistake, I shall simply answer them by saying, 'Comrades, in our business he who does not make any mistakes is not working!'"

That was a fatuous notion, of course, but there were times when Popov could compound bad judgment by being stubborn. In mid-November CIA officers in Berlin reported to Washington as follows: "Significant in Subject's reaction to the Mili investigation was the total absence of any desire to [seek asylum in the United States] to save his skin. . . . If we desire [him to do so] we will have to exert tremendous pressure on Subject." The "tremendous pressure" certainly could and should have been exerted, but it wasn't. The last meeting with him took place on 17 November 1958. It was not much different from many others, although there were, of course, forebodings as to what the Moscow visit might presage. Popov nevertheless devoted a great deal of time to discussing trivia, such as whether to take along presents to his friends in Russia. After some discussion he decided not to do so. Instead, he would take people out to dinner once he arrived. "I have a reserve of one thousand East marks put away with my wife. She is saving it to buy a couch." He would use that money to take his most useful contacts out to dinner at one of Moscow's most expensive restaurants.

DENOUEMENT

Pyotr Semyonovich Popov was never again seen in the West. What happened when he returned to Moscow in late 1958? Several CIA contacts were made with him there; during the first, made in early January 1959, Popov passed a note containing good quality information and the news that he had been dismissed from the GRU, placed in the reserves, and was awaiting reassignment. According to subsequently received information this action was taken at KGB insistence to deny him access to GRU information while giving the KGB time to determine how the Americans would handle the case in Moscow and whether Popov had any accomplices.

After several subsequent CIA contacts, a meeting was held in Moscow in September 1959 during which Popov courageously passed a secure message that told of his arrest in February 1959 and of KGB control of subsequent meetings. Continuation of contact had been allowed by the KGB in order to secure other GRU activities that he was in a position to compromise. Finally, in October 1959, having achieved that objective, the KGB, with great publicity, arrested Popov and detained his CIA contact after an encounter on a Moscow bus. The CIA officer was held briefly and then declared persona non grata.[8] The Soviets later announced that Popov was tried, sentenced to death, and shot.

What had brought Popov under Soviet suspicion? Several of his own actions could have aroused Soviet suspicion regarding his loyalty. Other authors have suggested additional possible contributing factors, and some have contradicted each other in their speculation about his demise.[9] Without having special access to classified information on this aspect of the case, I will leave the definitive counterintelligence analysis of the case to the experts. In any case, in my view Popov died unnecessarily, not only because of his own stubbornness and false confidence in insisting on returning to Moscow but also because of the inability of his CIA masters to thwart that action.

APPRECIATION

The essence of the Popov miracle was what intelligence operators call "access." This is a crucial term; no matter how brilliant the spy, if he does not have access to secrets he will be of no use. Popov initially demonstrated an instinct for grasping the CIA's interests in intelligence in his first offering of information. Thereafter, in addition to responding to specific guidance and requirements, on his own initiative he obtained information that proved to be of considerable importance—all because he had access that he manipulated to his and the CIA's advantage.

To put Popov's contribution in perspective, remember the timeframe of his activities: 1953 to late 1958. U-2 photographic intelligence was a relatively new creation, and satellite photography was still only on the drawing board. Nevertheless, the Cold War was at its height. Ever since Stalin's death in 1953 Khrushchev had been engaged in a ruthless struggle with other surviving members of the former leader's coterie, while at the same time pursuing aggressive policies abroad that eventually led to the Cuban Missile Crisis. In the United States John Foster Dulles was the energetic and highly articulate secretary of state who consistently encouraged his younger brother, CIA Director Allen Dulles, to use both fair means and foul in "rolling back the Iron Curtain." NATO had been in existence since 1949 but West Germany, the very heart of NATO's area, didn't became a member until 1955. Anyone who served in Europe during World War II and witnessed firsthand the ruthless power of the Soviet Army, like many of us who later joined the CIA, was bound to fear that NATO defenses were still insufficient.

In these circumstances a senior Soviet officer such as Pyotr Popov, functioning within a major intelligence headquarters where he had access to highly classified Soviet military documents, was bound to be worth a considerable effort. Unfortunately, to those of us who had known and liked him, Popov—despite the encouragement and compliments of his case officers—was not in a position to appreciate the full extent of his contribution to the U.S. intelligence effort.

2
Oleg Penkovsky
In Quest of Honor

THE APOSTASY

The business of espionage is a catalog of surprises, and no one could have been in greater contrast to Pyotr Popov than the man to whom we now turn. Look for a moment at a letter, dated some two years after Popov's death, hand carried to London in April 1961 by an Englishman named Greville Wynne. Written in Cyrillic Russian, the letter had been neatly typed on a single sheet of paper. Immediately turned over to the British and U.S. intelligence services, this is how it began:

To Her Majesty Queen of Great Britain, Elizabeth II
To Mr. MacMillan

To Mr. Kennedy   *To Mr. Eisenhower*
To Mr. Nixon   *To Mr. Herter*
To Mr. Johnson   *To Mr. Gates*
To Mr. Rusk   *To Mr. Brucker*
To Mr. McNamara   *To Mr. A. Dulles*

My dear Queen,
My dear President,
My dear Gentlemen,

In my first letter of 19th July 1960, I have already told you that I
have reappraised my place in life and about my decision and readi-
ness to devote myself to the Cause of a struggle for a true, just and
free world for humanity. For this Cause I will fight to the end.

I ask you to consider me as your soldier. Henceforth the ranks
of your Armed Forces are increased by one man.

You can have no doubts about my devotion, steadfastness, self-
lessness and resolution in the battle for your Cause (which is also
mine). You will always be satisfied with me, you will always
remember me with a good word. Your acknowledgement—I will
earn it. For this a great deal of time will not be necessary . . .

This phenomenal letter had been written by Oleg Vladimirovich
Penkovsky, a Russian army colonel stationed in Moscow who had for
some time been trying to enlist as "a soldier-warrior for the cause of
Truth, for the ideals of a truly free world and of Democracy for
Mankind"—as a spy, in other words, because espionage was the only
weapon available to him. Unfortunately for Penkovsky, volunteering
as a spy for the West had not been an easy thing to do in the Moscow
of 1960, where even foreigners residing in or visiting Russia were
hypersensitive to the dangers of betrayal and the repressive authorities
of the Soviet Union were feared by all.

Yet the man who wrote the letter was utterly sincere, and enor-
mously frustrated because no Westerner would accept him at face
value. Oleg Penkovsky was, on the surface at least, most of the things
Pyotr Popov was not. He was a well-educated, articulate, and fairly
cosmopolitan man who possessed a pre-Revolutionary upper-class
heritage that he (and the Soviets) never forgot. Unlike most Russians,

Penkovsky spoke fairly good English and had it not been for his lineage, which once discovered was an indelible black mark against him in the Soviet system, he almost certainly would have become a general officer in the Soviet Army. Before his background came to the attention of the KGB he had already achieved the rank of full colonel at the age of thirty, and with it a position that would have fulfilled the most extravagant dreams of all but a few other Soviet citizens.

Above all Penkovsky was dynamic and aggressive. An American businessman who dealt with him in Paris in 1961 said that he "hit like a cyclone." Indeed, it was in a way very much like a cyclone that he came to the attention of the American and British governments. Penkovsky's decision to cooperate clandestinely with the West against his own country was for him not a difficult one; he was driven compulsively to do so. Establishing contact with a responsible American or Englishman through whom he could actually initiate cooperation was, on the other hand, excruciatingly complex, because like almost everyone in the Soviet Union in the 1950s and 1960s, including foreigners, he lived in continual apprehension of the KGB.

Diplomats from all the leading countries resided in Moscow, in addition to a number of Westerners traveling in the Soviet Union, usually for business or study. For a Russian to make their acquaintance was troublesome, and gaining their confidence was even more so. "Last August," Penkovsky later recounted, "I was in Odessa on leave with my wife and daughter. On my way back to Moscow from Kiev I found myself in a railroad car in which were American students and instructors in the Russian language [who were also American]. I could not approach them, however, because there was an Armenian with them who is known to be a KGB informant." On other occasions, he said, "I stalked the American Embassy like a wolf, looking for a reliable foreigner, a patriot. . . . I even went to the America House [a U. S. dormitory and recreation facility for the Marine guards] where I could see them inside playing cards and drinking whiskey, and there was a militiaman [a Soviet policeman] at the entrance. I waited for some American to come out so I could contact him and say, 'Mister, you are a patriot. Please deliver this letter to your embassy. Everything in it is self-explanatory.' But I couldn't meet anyone. No one came out."

The letter Penkovsky had written to pass to the American Embassy was similar to the one quoted earlier. Apprehensive at having it in his pocket, Penkovsky likened it to an "atom bomb":

> I even sat, with this bomb . . . across the street from the American
> Embassy [where] there is a tunnel-like archway and two benches. I
> sat there for a long time, smoking. . . . I'll tell you why.
> . . . There is a new building opposite your embassy. . . . There is a
> [KGB] safe house there from which photographs are taken, auto-
> matically on a movie strip, of all those who walk through the
> gates, all those who drive in and out, and all those who hang
> around for a long time. . . . You people drive out almost exclusive-
> ly. The car drives swiftly, eight cylinders, it is gone, gone and can-
> not be caught up with, not even by taxi.
> I am sitting on a bench. . . . I can be there because across from
> your embassy is the Moscow River. I walk on that side, enter a
> store, look at materials.

Trying to appear casual as he waits for an American to come out, he sizes up the people who emerge because an *important* U.S. citizen would be most useful. "When Americans come out whom the militia-man salutes, these are the permanent diplomats. Those who do not have diplomatic passports, or the casual visitors coming to the con-sular section, he does not greet."

From time to time he spots someone emerging who has both been saluted and looks promising. "I walk out of the store, or get up from the bench. There goes the man on the other side. I do not cross the street because I fear being photographed from the safe house. I walk along the street parallel to him." Then suddenly the American gets into a taxi, and is gone. Penkovsky's effort has been wasted. "I once followed an American to the Bolshoi Theater, and wanted to go up and say, 'I have a request.' But he would have called a militiaman. So instead I walked on, and I was afraid."

At long last, at eleven o'clock on the night of 12 August 1960, along the dark banks of the Moscow River, Penkovsky made his long-hoped-for contact, with a distinctive red-bearded American out for an evening stroll with a fellow tourist. By coincidence, Penkovsky realized, he had seen the pair on the train from Kiev. The bland prose of an embassy memorandum describes the event:

> Shortly after midnight last night Mr. Eldon Ray Cox, an American tourist, requested at the Marine Desk to talk to an American Embassy official. Basic information from Cox, who is twenty-six years of age, is as follows:
>
> At 11 P.M. last night, while Cox and a group of fellow tourists were walking away from Red Square toward the river, a Soviet citizen approached them and started a conversation. The Soviet citizen is described by Cox as being about forty years of age, of medium build, about 5′9″.
>
> Cox, who speaks Russian, detected a Ukrainian accent.

As the group walked along the bridge, the Soviet walked along with them and told Cox and his colleague, "I beg you to help me." . . .This Soviet citizen claims to be an infantry officer who formerly was a Communist but is no longer one. He speaks English fairly well. . . . He further claims that he has been carrying two letters since mid-July but has not been able to give them to anyone. As Cox was walking along the bank of the Moscow River talking with him, the Soviet furtively gave him the two enclosed letters and requested that they be brought immediately to the embassy.

The embassy officer who interviewed Cox had no help to offer, but concluded their meeting with a severe admonition to reject all future contacts of this type.

Penkovsky's letter, when read by senior diplomats at the embassy, was dismissed as probable "provocation" attributable to some branch of the Soviet government. ("Provocations" were actions carried out, usually by the KGB, to place U.S. diplomats, as well as citizens of other non-Communist countries, in politically compromising situations. From the Soviet standpoint provocations were useful in making diplomats so cautious that at times they were almost immobilized—as they were in this case.) Typically, the only action taken by the embassy was to forward Penkovsky's letter to Washington, where the State Department passed it to the CIA.

In one of the letters handed to Cox, Penkovsky wrote:

> I have at my disposal very important materials on many subjects of great importance to your government. . . . I request that you pass the following to appropriate authorities of the United States. . . .
>
> I wish to pass these materials to you immediately for study, analysis, and subsequent utilization. . . . It is desirable that the transfer be effected, not through personal contact, but through a dead drop. . . .
>
> Your reply: Please inform me (preferably in the Russian language) through my dead drop No. 1 (see its description and manner of use concerning the manner, form, time, and place for passing of the indicated material).
>
> After you receive the material from me, it would be desirable to arrange a personal meeting with your representative. . . .
>
> I ask that in working with me you observe all the rules of [espionage] tradecraft and security, and not permit any slip-up. Protect me.

In Washington, as in Moscow, the response to Penkovsky's initiative was near-paralysis. The American ambassador in Moscow quickly made known his views: he was opposed to any response whatever to this initiative, and he was not alone. The recent U-2 disaster had created a climate in which caution was the watchword. What if Penkovsky's approach proved part of a plan to further embarrass the United States?

Earlier in 1960 the United States had been caught red-handed when a U-2 aircraft on a photographic reconnaissance mission over the Soviet Union was shot down by the Russians. The United States at first claimed that the flight was intended to collect meteorological information, but that story did not stand up because the pilot, Francis Gary Powers, was caught and under KGB pressure admitted that he was a spy. Premier Khrushchev thereupon canceled a scheduled visit to the Soviet Union by President Dwight Eisenhower. It is only fair to say that since both diplomats and intelligence people are paid to imagine worst-case scenarios, this new development gave them good reason to proceed cautiously from that moment on.

Several weeks went by without any response to Penkovsky. He was not, however, the type to sit idly by, and fortunately he had a wealth of connections. By late 1960 Penkovsky had been assigned to the State Committee for Science and Technology (GNTK), an organization devoted to gathering industrial information from the scientifically advanced nations and staffed with genuine technical specialists but also seeded heavily with intelligence officers. Penkovsky's official duties there included relations with a number of foreign businessmen visiting the USSR.

In mid-December a distinguished British metallurgist, Dr. A. D. Merriman, delivered a learned address on "The Thermodynamic Process in Steel-making" to a group of Soviet "experts"; Merriman was somewhat disappointed to note, from the questions posed by the audience, that few if any of the "experts" present really understood what he was talking about. After the meeting, however, "a rather friendly Russian-type" named Penkovsky took him in hand, and returned with him to his hotel along with another Brit. As the three men enjoyed a drink at the bar Penkovsky asked Merriman if he had any spare cigarettes. It was not an unusual question because cigarettes were in short supply, and foreign brands were especially prized. When Merriman said yes, they proceeded to his hotel room to get a few packs from his suitcase.

Once in the room, however, Penkovsky seemed to lose all interest in tobacco. Instead he locked the door, turned the radio up as loud as possible, and produced from his pocket a folded pack of papers wrapped in cellophane. In a whisper he told Merriman that these were secret documents he wanted to put in the hands of the American Embassy. He stressed that he could not turn them over to Merriman, only to an American official. He asked the Englishman to make a call to the American Embassy, requesting that an appropriate person be sent immediately to the hotel room.

Merriman, sensitive to the dangers of being compromised while visiting a police state, refused to cooperate or even touch the papers; Penkovsky, after pleading with him briefly, resignedly put them back in his pocket and departed. He did not seem angry or offended as he left Merriman's room, and though he was "around and underfoot" for the remainder of the metallurgist's visit, he gave no sign of wanting to raise the matter a second time.

A few days later, however, when Merriman was at the Moscow airport preparing to leave for London, the CIA record states that, "Penkovsky showed up about five minutes before departure time. He called Merriman aside, asking him to get word to appropriate American officials in London that Penkovsky would be waiting at his home telephone (717 184) every Sunday at 10 A.M. for a call; all the American representative had to do was ring that number; after that he would receive further instructions." Merriman remained cautiously noncommittal, but once he returned to Britain he alerted the British and American authorities that this maverick Russian would be hard to stop. After every rejection he would find a new way to present his case.

Another British businessman who had been present at Merriman's meetings with Penkovsky remembered that, on the first occasion especially, Penkovsky showed signs of considerable nervous tension; at one point he was almost in tears. Merriman's colleague thought that if Penkovsky's offer was not a genuine one then Penkovsky was a very good actor. Penkovsky had offered secrets of Soviet rocket propulsion in exchange for American help in getting himself and his family safely out to the West. Penkovsky's wife, who accompanied her husband to a dinner given by the British delegation of which Merriman and his colleague were a part, was a cultured woman who spoke excellent French. She seemed to have a close understanding with her husband, and thus knew what he was up to. Despite the influence of British Embassy briefings about Soviet provocation, the pair interpreted Penkovsky's convincing performance as that of a desperate man.

Because of the number of Britons Penkovsky had been meeting in Moscow, the CIA now queried the British authorities for any information they might have on him. The British thereupon produced a brief report from their military attaché in Ankara, Turkey, where Penkovsky had at one time been stationed. This report described him as "pleasant and well-mannered, 5′9″, slender; iron-gray hair; 160 lbs.; Western appearance." Somewhat more perceptive was the following observation: "Whenever I met Penkovsky, I noticed [that] the genial and smiling expression on his face fades when one leaves him, and is replaced by a rather weak and almost frightened look."

By now CIA officials in Washington were determined to respond to Penkovsky's approach. The chief of the agency's Soviet Division, John Maury, was a patrician from an old Virginia family who despised cowardice in any form. He was, moreover, a brilliant, realistic, and scholarly man who, as a U.S. Marine colonel, had served in the Soviet Union during World War II. Sensitive to Penkovsky's plight, and believing it likely that he was a genuine defector, Maury was willing to defy the cautious American ambassador in Moscow who in no

way wanted his embassy involved. As to the view of the embassy security officer that Penkovsky's actions were "a provocation," Maury
dismissed it contemptuously and decided that the CIA would join the
braver British in dealing with Penkovsky.

Efforts were still under way to arrange a clandestine meeting
between Penkovsky and a CIA representative when the ever-frenetic
Russian colonel made still another contact of his own devising. A
Canadian business delegation, headed by Dr. J. M. Harrison, had visited Moscow in mid-January 1961. Upon his return to Ottawa, Dr.
Harrison recalled his meetings with Penkovsky: "He is a man of about
forty-two years . . . and has seen a little of how the other half of the
world lives. . . . He speaks English rather badly, but nevertheless intel-
ligently, and has a rather smooth, urbane appearance. He dresses
smartly in the Western manner, insofar as Russian tailoring permits."
Because Penkovsky was in charge of arrangements for Harrison's visit,
the two men had ample opportunity to see each other alone, and the
Russian seized the occasion to ask Harrison to arrange a contact for
him with William Van Vliet of the Canadian Trade Commission in
Moscow. "I suggested it could be done through the Canadian
Embassy," Harrison wrote later, "but he apparently wanted to meet
privately in my room. This puzzled me a bit but I agreed to see what
could be done."

When the meeting finally took place it was a repeat of other similar meetings Penkovsky had engineered, with the telephone being
quickly disconnected, warnings issued about official eavesdropping,
the radio kept on very loud, and voices lowered to a whisper. The purpose of this contact was a request that Van Vliet deliver an envelope
to someone at the U.S. Embassy. The Canadian, perhaps too surprised
to refuse, stuck the envelope in his pocket. "I saw Van Vliet the night
before I left Moscow," Harrison wrote, and "he then told me that the
envelope was sealed with scotch tape, was quite fat, and was unad-
dressed. Penkovsky may, if he comes to Canada, consider defecting.

He has a wife and child in Moscow, but is warming up to another woman. This could provide a convenient rationalization for abandoning his wife. . . . If he does come to Canada," Harrison concluded, "I hope to learn about it ahead of time so that I can be somewhere other than where he is!"

The CIA in Washington was dismayed by Penkovsky's latest initiative, but shortly thereafter came better news. A British commercial delegation led by an Englishman named Greville Wynne had been visiting Moscow—with all arrangements being handled by Penkovsky. At a party for Wynne held on 10 March 1961, Penkovsky told the British commercial counselor that the Soviets were planning to send to England a delegation of their own, and Penkovsky underlined that he would be the delegation's leader. Evidently his pride was deeply involved because he emphasized that though he spoke English, he was not to be considered a mere interpreter.

As it happened Greville Wynne had been recently co-opted into the ranks of British intelligence. When he sent word to London of Penkovsky's visit, the news was quickly passed to the CIA in Washington and arrangements were made for meetings to be held between both intelligence services and this intriguing Russian during his London visit. In Moscow, meanwhile, events were proceeding on a separate track because the impatient Penkovsky could not wait for the London meetings, scheduled for late April. Wynne, still in Moscow, therefore found himself under continuous pressure to immediately transmit purloined documents to the British authorities.

On 6 April Penkovsky came to Wynne's hotel room where, after his by-now ritualized security precautions, he showed Wynne a secret pocket in his trousers that he then slit open with a razor blade. From it he produced a bundle of papers and asked Wynne to take them back to England. The Englishman, objecting to their bulk, at first stalled but finally agreed to take two of the documents, which he selected at random. Poor Wynne did not realize what faced him next. Not wanting to keep the papers on his person, he took them to the British Embassy for safekeeping. Unfortunately, because it was a holiday there were no diplomatic officers present, so he asked the British guard on duty for an envelope, sealed the papers in it, and wrote "To be called for by Mr. Wynne" across the front. The guard promised to keep the envelope in a drawer of his desk.

The next morning Wynne returned to the embassy, recovered his envelope, and asked to see the British Ambassador, whom he previously had met in connection with his delegation's business. A secretary informed him, however, that the ambassador was too busy to meet with him. Wynne's protest that he wanted to discuss an important security question, not a mere commercial matter, did not work, and he left the embassy aware that he carried papers which, if discovered on his person by the Soviets, would certainly have resulted in a heavy criminal penalty. Yet, having been turned away by the British Embassy, he now had no place to put them for safekeeping.

As often happened, Penkovsky meanwhile had gone along temporarily with a partial response to one of his requests, only to push for full compliance later. On 12 April, after driving Wynne to the airport and with only twenty minutes before boarding time, he beckoned the Englishman to the toilets, made sure all the stalls were empty, then said, "Mr. Wynne, you must now decide whether to trust me. There is no more time. Take the package of remaining papers." Then, as the Englishman displayed reluctance, he added "If not, the least you can do is take this sheet."

Despite his misgivings, since the plane was ready for departure Wynne finally accepted the single sheet of paper proffered him and, as they embraced, Russian-fashion, Penkovsky said with tears in his eyes, "You don't know how much you have done for your country, and for me!" The "single sheet" that Wynne brought back to London and handed over to the intelligence authorities there was the letter to Queen Elizabeth and President Kennedy. The letter consisted of certain personal requests that were certainly not unreasonable considering the risks Penkovsky had already taken and would continue to take in the future. Extravagant as some of his language may seem, it truly mirrored his feelings and to the end he proved a man of his word. In addition to the portion quoted above, Penkovsky wrote:

> *I have certain personal requests.*
> *I request that you look into the question of making me, from this moment on, a citizen of the U.S.A. or of Great Britain. I also ask you to grant me at your discretion a military rank in the Army of the U.S.A. I have sufficient knowledge and experience and not only now but also in the future I will be able to be of real benefit to you while working in the U.S.A. itself, a prospect of which I constantly dream.*
>
> *Secondly, I ask that you give instructions that proper precautions be taken during the careful, deliberate, and conspiratorial work with me conducted by your workers.*
>
> *Thirdly, at this time I am handing over a number of materials which I have gathered over the last year. I ask you to direct their assessment, as well as a decision on a fixed sum for this work. I have no special savings and money will be necessary in the future. I ask you to put the sum which is granted to me in an American bank.*
>
> *These are my personal requests.*
>
> *Once again I assure you of my boundless love and respect for you, for the American people, and for all those who find themselves under your Banner. I believe in your Cause. I am ready to fulfill any of your orders. I await them.*

THE NEW COMMITMENT

"Operation proceeding as planned. First meeting with Penkovsky expected late this evening." The CIA cable from London to Washington both surprised and delighted those who had been following the unusual case. It announced that Oleg Penkovsky would arrive in Britain on 20 April 1961 as head of a Soviet delegation. The case officers could at last take measure of this extraordinary man who had been so persistent in trying to assist America and Britain, despite continual rebuffs.

The first encounter took place in a room at a central London hotel, the sort of large and bustling establishment where almost anyone can remain anonymous if he wishes. One of the case officers assigned to this case (all of them Soviet specialists) was George Kisevalter, the same bilingual Russian-American who had dealt with Pyotr Popov in Vienna and Berlin. A decision had been made to give Penkovsky free rein to talk about whatever was on his mind during the first meeting. After that the conversations that took place in London as well as in several other British cities (as the delegation toured the provinces) soon developed into serious and orderly debriefing sessions. Nevertheless, Penkovsky was an unusually voluble man and random digressions repeatedly occurred. At the time regretted by the case officers involved, who were under heavy pressure to satisfy high priority intelligence requirements, it is precisely these digressions that enable us to piece together a fuller picture of this unusual man and why he chose to work against his own country.

From the time of his birth Oleg Penkovsky had enjoyed most of the advantages that the Soviet system had to offer. His favored position never stemmed, however, from being of "proletarian" parentage. Quite the contrary. He was proud of his upper-class origins, excellent education, and better-than-average means. Despite the attempts made after the Revolution to deprive Russians of any wealth accumulated during Tsarist times, it appears that either by accident or design his mother was able to conserve some of the family's small fortune. When talking to his British and American contacts Penkovsky made no secret of his personal advantages.

Penkovsky's father had been killed in 1919, the same year Oleg was born. At the time of his death the senior Penkovsky had been fighting as a member of one of the so-called White Armies, a number of which attempted unsuccessfully to wrest power from the Bolsheviks (usually subsidized by Britain or America). Fortunately for the younger Penkovsky, whatever record there was of the circumstances of his father's death while fighting with an anti-Communist army did not emerge for many years. By the time they did—as the result of a long, systematic research effort by the KGB—Penkovsky was already an extremely well-connected colonel in the Soviet Army. For some time, however, and thanks to a fine combat record, marriage to a general's daughter, and friendship with other extremely high-ranking officers, his career was not adversely affected by his family background. Nor was it at first thoroughly investigated.

Although he had to be secretive about it, Penkovsky was nevertheless proud of his ancestry. Seven paragraphs into the transcript of the first meeting in London finds him talking at length about his origins: "I was born in the Caucasus. My father was a lieutenant in the Tsarist Army, and my grandfather had been a well-known jurist. Only recently have I been accused by the Soviet authorities of coming from a background of nobility. My mother brought me up alone. I was the only son, and my father disappeared without a trace."

Forever tense, during this first meeting Penkovsky spoke in rapid-fire and sometimes incomplete sentences, frequently digressing to the subject of his family: "My father was well-born, he was a mining engineer. . . . I hardly ever saw him, and never called him Father. . . . I was four months old when he last held me in his arms, and he never saw me again."

Penkovsky had one highly placed living relative, Valentin Antonovich Penkovsky, a career army officer who had been imprisoned at the time of Stalin's sweeping purge of the military in 1937. Fortunately this uncle had not been executed as so many of his peers had; along with others fortunate enough to survive he was restored to active duty when Germany attacked the Soviet Union and the army had been rapidly expanded to meet the new threat. Many senior, experienced commanders suddenly found that, instead of being pariahs, they were now in great demand. "He now commands the Far Eastern Military District," Penkovsky said in wonderment. "Colonel-General Penkovsky! He is my great-uncle, but since he knows about our past, he doesn't keep in touch with me. I see him on rare occasions, [but] he ignores me because of our noble background. When occasionally we meet, he says 'How are you?' but nothing more."

Whatever his great-uncle's feelings may have been, it was evident in everything the younger Penkovsky said and did that he considered himself a member of an upper stratum of society. During one meeting, in going over a Moscow town plan with his case officers and trying to pinpoint the locations of important official installations, his attention fell on the location of his own flat. "And here is where *Gospodin* [Mister] Penkovsky lives!" he exclaimed; "not *Tovarishch* [Comrade]!" With his foreign friends he thus insisted on a form of address reserved in the Soviet Union for foreign capitalists.

In a professedly classless society Penkovsky had little use for the myth of equality. If anything he himself was living proof that, even though the Revolution and the Stalin era had drastically changed the demography of the Soviet Union, the love of status and material possessions among the Communist hierarchy represented a continuation of pre-Revolutionary tradition. Penkovsky's own acquisitiveness soon became evident. "You know," he said at one point, "I'd like to walk around London a bit. . . . There are many fine things to see in the stores, and my wife has given me a whole list of things to get. There are beautiful vases made of porcelain. They cost about ten pounds. When I was a regimental commander we liberated a porcelain-manu-facturing town—the center of the industry in Czechoslovakia—and brought home all kinds of porcelain vases and other items. They even presented crystal vases to [Marshal of the Soviet Union Ivan] Konev and me. Anyway, I have many expensive things at home, including rugs from Turkey, and I live on a high scale, for Communism."

During his visits to Western Europe Penkovsky's purchases came to be recognized as a constant problem for his case officers. A report based on a debriefing of Greville Wynne says that, "Penkovsky took back among other things from Paris two red ruffled ladies' umbrellas for his wife and daughter, which would have stood out in Moscow as probably the only ones in the city. He himself was the only official in the GNTK to wear white nylon shirts, a rarity in those days; and, to make matters worse, he acquired a duplicate of Wynne's old-school necktie, which he wore with great pride, perhaps not understanding that only attendance at a particular British school would have entitled him to do so." Wynne had to feign anger and threaten to go tieless before Penkovsky would renounce this attractive symbol.

Penkovsky's craving for possessions was equaled only by his liking for women, with whom his relations were always those of a *grand seigneur*. As he told his case officers, "I like to live freely, and now and then take a lady out. I know how to approach them and never drink to excess." He also confessed that he had expensive habits, and Wynne's testimony certainly bore this out: "On one occasion," says a 1965 report, "Wynne carried in [to the Soviet Union] two gold wrist watches for Penkovsky, one of which Penkovsky immediately gave to a shop girl at a greengrocery on Gorki Street." Many of his purchases were, however, things unavailable in Russia, such as "an entire suite of furniture for our apartment."

Penkovsky's extravagant purchases were not made simply on behalf of himself and his immediate family, however; it soon became obvious that they played a real role in assuring his access to key members of the Soviet ruling class. "I swear by my daughter and my future work with you," he explained, "that I must do the following. I must bring each and every friend of mine some small item, since they know that I am going abroad. It does not have to be an expensive item in every case, but it would be extremely bad [manners] to neglect anyone." To do Penkovsky justice, it does appear that during this period it was indeed considered a social obligation of those privileged Russians who were allowed to travel abroad to bring home presents to less-traveled friends and family members (remember that Popov had felt the same obligation). If in this respect Penkovsky was more extravagant than the norm, it can only be said that he was also unusual in every other aspect of politics, politeness, and pleasure.

A parenthetical note in the transcript of one of the London meetings reads as follows: "Subject listed a long and wide variety of items such as fountain pens, neckties, ladies' nail polish, lipstick, and a gamut of medicine for just run-of-the-mill friends, and more expensive items for influential friends such as marshals of the Soviet Union, generals, and colonels. His elaborate notebook, which included outlines of his wife's and daughter's feet as well as magazine clippings of all conceivable fine ladies' wear, also contained a request from a certain Obolentsov, chief administrator to [a ranking general in the Air Force.]"

It is quite possible that his extravagance and toadying were also motivated, in part at least, by Penkovsky's insecurity stemming from the dreaded secret of his bourgeois heritage. One cannot be overly sanctimonious about the manners and morals of a man who lives in imminent threat of sanctions for the very fact that his father was a member of the upper class. Nor should it be forgotten that in considerable measure Penkovsky's success as our secret agent came through the contacts he made throughout the upper strata of Soviet government. Explaining why he must bring a present to the secretary of a well-known official named Gvishiani, he said, "He is my chief, he is married to the daughter of Kosygin [Soviet prime minister under Brezhnev]. Gvishiani's father was a lieutenant general in the KGB." In referring to these highly placed people Penkovsky was talking about his own life insurance. It turned out that in the end the amount spent on him and by him was calculated to be infinitesimal compared to the value of the intelligence he produced.

THE MAKING OF A DEFECTOR

Though sometimes a calculated affectation, Penkovsky's conviviality was nonetheless real. He craved people, and his gregariousness was facilitated by the very fact of being well connected. In turn in large part his connections were the product of having been, from the beginning of his military career, a highly effective officer. Penkovsky received his commission in the artillery in 1939 upon completion of a two-year course. In the beginning he was no different from many others who joined the national Communist youth organization. "I considered myself a progressive young man of our country fighting for the ideas of Lenin. My ambition then was to join the Party and in 1939 I was already a candidate for membership."

He found himself going on active duty at a time when, as a result of massive purges, there was more than usual room for advancement. The purges were carried out by Nikolai Yezhov, head of the People's Commissariat for Internal Affairs (NKVD), whose genocidal mania equaled Hitler's. Penkovsky was thus part of a generation of officers commissioned to replace those who had perished, not in action against the enemy but as a result of Communist paranoia.

By this time Hitler had crushed the Polish Army, though he had not yet fully occupied all of Poland. Stalin was wary, like all Russian rulers, of having a potential enemy on his borders, and decided to extend his frontier defenses into the area not yet under German dominion. In Soviet parlance this action was known euphemistically as the "liberation of the Ukraine" because the area of Poland thus preempted was largely populated by Ukrainian speakers. During this time of flux Penkovsky became one of many "political commissars" that were needed to handle Communist political indoctrination and maintain the discipline of the rapidly expanding military force within newly occupied territories. No wonder, for in connection with the Stalin-Yezhov purges it is estimated that at least twenty thousand Communist Party political workers had been imprisoned and in many cases executed.[1] Penkovsky therefore began his active military career in a particularly broad capacity, as both a political shepherd of those less educated and articulate than he and as a combat officer. The potential advantage of such a dual function within the Soviet system is indicated by the fact that, at a much higher rank, Khrushchev was to achieve fame as the overall political-military disciplinarian of Soviet forces in the Ukraine.

After the Ukraine came Finland. "In January 1940 our division was sent into action there . . . and within two days [it] was decimated. Only 10 percent survived. All the regimental commanders were killed. I was fortunate to escape without a scratch [because] I was an artillery officer, and our positions are somewhat behind the front lines. Despite the hardships, I was still full of enthusiasm and, as the war ended, I was accepted into the Party." These words of Penkovsky in translation and on paper seem coldly objective, but the printed page is misleading; those who talked to him in person often found him agitated and tense. No wonder, for much of his adult life had been a bundle of conflicts and contradictions, as momentary glory quickly faded into disaster, disappointment, and, in his mind, dishonor.

One of the many minor ironies of Penkovsky's life was that he had met his wife because her father, Lieutenant General Gapanovich, was a leading political figure and member of the so-called Military Council, and was among those who ruled the city of Moscow. In his capacity as a political commissar Penkovsky had met the general, whom he described in glowing terms as "a very fine man; he helped me a great deal, and he liked me. He saw that [politically] I was very enthusiastic, which was quite true at that time, and I do not deny this to you. I only make this remark now to explain why later I changed all my views. . . . I worked for Gapanovich until November 1943. At that time the recapture of Kiev was being celebrated and I thought the war would end very soon. Here I was, with no distinctions or decorations. I received nothing for the Finnish campaign, only a commendation and a cigarette case." At least a thousand men had already been awarded the coveted title of Hero of the Soviet Union, but Penkovsky was not one of them. "I therefore submitted a request for front line duty, and was sent again to the Ukraine." That immense area was now being invaded by the Germans, and Penkovsky's career as a political worker ended when he was named deputy commander of an artillery regiment.

On the Ukrainian front Penkovsky distinguished himself in a number of ways. As an artillery officer he was uncompromising, to the point of twice shooting junior officers with his own revolver when he found them inciting the troops to desert in the face of enemy fire. The first incident occurred in December 1943 when, in Penkovsky's words, a captain "proved himself a coward and not only started to run away, but began calling on other officers to join him, and to get all the infantry to follow them." His firm action prevented a rout, however, and Penkovsky was praised by his commander. The other incident took place in March 1944 when Penkovsky shot an infantry lieutenant who, after acting as an observer for Penkovsky's artillery, started to run away with his whole platoon even before the advancing enemy tanks were within range. Again, his draconian firmness "stopped the panic."

Three months later, in June 1944, a crucial event that would materially influence Penkovsky's future life took place. He was about to leave a military hospital after two months spent recovering from wounds when he heard that his former commander, Marshal Varentsov, had been badly wounded. He knew that Varentsov's wife, mother, and two daughters were having trouble getting food and fuel, despite the marshal's lofty rank. "I therefore took care of the family, because he was a very nice person, and I knew he would reward me tenfold for anything I did." When the two men eventually returned together to the battle front, "Varentsov said, 'You are like a son to me.'"

As a direct result of the marshal's intercession Penkovsky was chosen to attend the Frunze Academy, Russia's West Point. That assignment was followed by two years at the Military-Diplomatic Academy,
where he was trained as an officer in the GRU. In early 1950 he was
promoted to full colonel. Ironically, from that apparently auspicious
moment on almost everything began to go wrong as his world
widened to include other nationalities, foreign lands, and greater challenges.

ANKARA

Penkovsky first came in contact with Americans when, in July 1955,
he was assigned to Ankara, Turkey, as acting military attaché and acting *rezident*. The latter term, in Russian, is synonymous with the CIA
term "chief of station" and in that capacity Penkovsky was to be temporarily in charge of GRU intelligence operations conducted from
Turkey's capital. Socially active as always, the Russian met a number
of Americans who were also serving in Turkey, but the one he remembered best and valued as a real friend was Col. Charles M. Peeke, the
U.S. military attaché. In the letter he later passed to the red-bearded
Cox as they walked along the Moscow River, Penkovsky asked to be
remembered to Peeke. He deeply valued his American, British, and
Canadian contacts, as implied during his third meeting in London,
when he asked what his American friends in Turkey thought of him.
The following is an excerpt from the transcript:

> **Penkovsky:** This is of interest to me. . . . Did the Americans give a
> good evaluation of me?
> **Kisevalter:** Yes, yes. Good. A brave, good chap.
> **P:** Is that what they reported?
> **K:** Yes, of course. Pleasant, friendly.
> **P:** That's good. . . . I had very good relations with the Americans. I
> wished them well.
> **K:** They felt that.

Referring to his eventually being withdrawn from Turkey by the Soviet Defense Ministry, he said, "If Peeke had been there at the time I would have contacted him. There were the usual doubts and struggle; I was searching my soul, but to Peeke I would have gone [defected]. Unfortunately he left, because his wife's mother had died." Penkovsky had been afraid of talking to the other Americans in Ankara, however, those whom he didn't know well. "But if Peeke had been there, I would have asked him, 'Give me an address for future contact.'" Those musings make clear that Penkovsky foresaw his undoing in Turkey, which resulted from the arrival in Ankara of a general as military attaché and *rezident,* after Penkovsky had occupied these positions in an acting capacity for five months.

It was a dark moment for him. "This General Savchenko arrived under the false name of Rubenko," Penkovsky explained. "He was an old man, over sixty years of age. I turned over everything to him." But along with the old general came Lieutenant Colonel Ionchenko, "who was very bitter against me. Since he had studied the Turkish language he was indignant that I, with English, had been sent as the deputy instead of himself. [He and the general] were dead set against me, and made my life miserable."

Meanwhile, said Penkovsky, Ionchenko "was simply approaching Turks in restaurants and offering them money to work for him. [He also attempted] to purchase military manuals from Turks in this crude manner. Naturally the Turkish counterintelligence, which was efficient, they noticed this. . . . Now, I will confess to you the following: my relations with the general and with Ionchenko were [so bad that] I made an anonymous telephone call from a public phone booth to the Turkish counterintelligence, informing them of Ionchenko's activities and specifying where his agent contacts were made." After a pause Penkovsky added, "By nature, I am a vengeful person. Having seen how unfairly I was treated, I had already decided to come over to you!"

Eventually Ionchenko was declared persona non grata by the Turkish authorities and returned to the Soviet Union. As Penkovsky explained, the reasons for the Turkish action resulted from a violation of GRU instructions by the general himself. "The shah and his wife were on a state visit and Turkish security and counterintelligence were on full alert to protect the visitors. We had instructions from the GRU chairman *not* under any circumstances to run operations during that time. Nevertheless, the general permitted Ionchenko to go out for an agent meeting [because it had already been scheduled]. . . . The incident [which led to Ionchenko's expulsion] actually occurred when a Turkish lieutenant was handing him a military manual. . . . I was sitting in the general's office when the embassy duty officer entered and said, 'Comrade General, your assistant has been detained by the Turkish counter-intelligence.' The general was terribly upset, and told me to go get him out of jail. I replied, 'Why did you let him go to this meeting?'"

There followed a furious argument between Penkovsky and the general because Savchenko was preparing to lie to Moscow in his report of the incident. In his cable to Moscow the general stated that the Turks and Americans had engineered a "provocation" against Ionchenko, and that it was actually while he was purchasing fruit, not a military manual, that he had been seized. "I asked the general, 'Are you a Communist?' And when he said 'yes,' I asked him why, then, did he lie?" Penkovsky threatened to report the true facts to Moscow through another channel, and he was as good as his word. Going to the KGB office within the Soviet Embassy, he sent off his own version of events via that service's independent communication channel. In Moscow the cable was shown directly to Ivan Aleksandrovich Serov, the KGB chairman, who in turn showed it to Khrushchev. The latter, who never trusted anybody, yelled, "Which fool is the liar, Penkovsky or the general? Figure this out, report to me." "I received no reprimand," Penkovsky later commented, "whereas the general was severely reprimanded for incompetence by the defense minister, Marshal Zhukov." In due course General Savchenko was expelled from the GRU. Nevertheless, this incident of betrayal of a colleague was considered a serious blot on Penkovsky's own record, at least within the GRU itself. He was consequently returned to Moscow for reassignment.

Because no one likes a stool pigeon, upon his arrival at GRU headquarters Penkovsky found that the leadership there still support-ed his erstwhile chief in Ankara: "He had sent [to his colleagues in Moscow] all kinds of gifts, and of course they were drinking buddies. . . . So they were indignant that a 'snot-nosed' young colonel like me could have behaved this way with respect to a general; they assumed that I wanted to trip him up in order to take his place as military attaché in Turkey."

Did anyone stand up for Penkovsky? Apparently not. "Basically, they said, I had reason on my side, but I was wrong in having behaved in a hooligan manner. [As a result], no general in the GRU wanted to work with me because 'you are a tattle-tale. Furthermore, you went out of channels. Why did you report this to Serov? You disgraced us in the eyes of our Neighbors.' ["Neighbors" in GRU parlance meant the KGB, an organization generally disliked by military people.] "So, since no one wanted to work with me, what should I do? I went to Marshal Varentsov. He told me to wait awhile until things blew over. . . . For a long time, they kept me in the GRU reserves, then gave me intermittent assignments . . . and finally back to the reserves!"

RESERVES

Penkovsky's chance for revenge and restoration of his self-esteem came in late 1958. His rehabilitation was in no way due to having repented, nor in the least to mending his ways. That was not how things were accomplished in the Soviet Union. Rather, a change in luck came through the personal intervention of his former commander,

Chief Marshal of Artillery Varentsov, whom Penkovsky had helped nurse back to health during the war. At the recommendation of the chief marshal he had been assigned as "class leader" to the Dzerzhinsky Military Academy, which provided specialized training in the most modern of Soviet weapons, its missiles. Penkovsky's position as "leader" invested him with a certain authority, and he used it for quite unacademic purposes.

Penkovsky studied hard, but not out of patriotism. By this time he was no longer "full of enthusiasm" for the Soviet cause, nor did he see himself as a "progressive young man fighting for the ideas of Lenin." All that was long gone. "To be quite honest with you," he said in London,

> my disaffection with the whole political system began a long time ago. The whole set-up was one of demagoguery, and deceit of the people. I myself was thinking of becoming a soldier in a new army, to adopt a new people, to struggle for a new ideal, and in some measure to avenge my father and millions of other people who died so terribly. . . . I thought that words are, after all, just words. I myself should bring something tangible. . . . I had a certain amount of authority, including the privilege of taking books and classified lectures from the special *fond* [classified library] to wherever I could work independently. I would block the door by placing a chair under the knob and study by myself. I copied everything down and, not having a camera, this took a very long time. I did most of this writing in the evening, and wrote so much that I got a big corn on my finger.
>
> I did it all carefully, because I knew you would check every word and if it were perfect maybe I would get a decoration.

Upon graduation from the Dzerzhinsky Academy Penkovsky learned that a bright future appeared to be awaiting him. Serov, who had meanwhile moved from being chairman of the KGB to become head of the GRU, and to whom Penkovsky had sent the out-of-channels message from Ankara, now wanted to send Penkovsky to New Delhi as *rezident*. This was a major post, one in which he could hope for promotion to general officer rank.

Penkovsky was delighted and all set to leave when he was called in by a major general who was chief of the Personnel Directorate. "He questioned me about my father, saying that I claimed my father had simply died. I replied, 'I have never seen my father, and never received a piece of bread from him.'" The general said, "But evidently you have concealed the fact that your father was killed while fighting as an officer of a White Russian army."

In due course Penkovsky was able to allay somewhat the general's suspicions—if not completely, at least enough for the KGB to approve brief assignments abroad. He had his mother write a letter stating that she had never told her son the circumstances of his father's death; in fact, she implied, she had not known them herself. They had been married during the First World War, then during the Russian Revolution that followed she bore him a son. Shortly after that her husband left and disappeared without a trace. The KGB was willing, at least provisionally, to accept Penkovsky's story, though it would not clear him for assignment abroad as a *rezident*. Penkovsky reacted with deep resentment. "If I had [already] completed my twenty-five years of service necessary for retirement, they would have discharged me as politically unreliable." Instead he was allowed to continue working, but was carefully watched.

Regardless of the limitations placed on him, however, Penkovsky's new assignment had one great advantage: an essential element of his duties was to make contact with foreigners. At first these contacts were made in Moscow; later his responsibilities were extended to include brief visits to see people abroad. The one crucial contact continued to be Greville Wynne, whose overt activity was drumming up import-export connections with countries in the Soviet Bloc. The two seemed to have liked each other personally, and it was through Wynne that Penkovsky had sent a message saying that he wanted to meet with British intelligence when and if he could find an excuse for an official trip to England.

For once Penkovsky was lucky, for Serov had appointed him a deputy chief within the GNTK, a cover behind which Soviet emissaries could hide while collecting information on other countries' advanced technology. Typically the Soviets tried to do many of these operations clandestinely rather than by the mainly overt means favored by most other countries. Because of his appointment Penkovsky had an opportunity to lead a GNTK delegation abroad that was to remain in London for two weeks. In addition to supervising the delegation, the untiring Penkovsky would be meeting late into the night with a team of British and American intelligence officers set up specifically for this purpose. Thus, late one evening in April 1961 when Penkovsky entered the lobby of London's slightly down-at-heel Mount Royal Hotel, one of the greatest espionage operations in history was born. Moreover, no one could claim that Penkovsky did not sense the importance of this moment, for he lost no time in explaining to his hosts at the hotel, "I now consider myself a representative of the Free World. I am yours . . . your soldier, your warrior, ready to fulfill any missions you may assign me, now and in the future. I believe that I can serve you most usefully in place [that is, in his GRU job in Russia] for at least a year or two, particularly if I work under a specific directive set by you, to fulfill missions within my capability."

KHRUSHCHEV'S OFFENSIVE

Penkovsky's "capability" turned out to be almost boundless. To appreciate the eventual impact he had on both Washington and London, however, it is necessary to turn to the trials and tensions of the early sixties. A new U.S. president had taken over in January 1961, and U.S. foreign policy as a whole was in flux. While highly successful in Europe, America had overextended itself in peripheral areas such as Laos. Closer to home, Cuban exiles had landed in the Bay of Pigs on 17 April 1961, but the U.S. government chose at the last moment not to give them all the military support previously pledged.

Khrushchev, interpreting these events with the mind of a man whose whole life had been an unrelenting, no-holds-barred struggle for personal and national power, saw Washington as weak. Although he had engineered his own accession to the premiership in 1957, only recently had Khrushchev fully consolidated his position. Within the year, greedy for power, he had himself proclaimed "a leading architect of victory in World War II," he launched a new personality cult, and he focused on being ready to take on the Soviet Union's "main enemy" (his term for the United States). The anti-American effort would not, however, involve a frontal attack; it would be carried out by indirection. Khrushchev began by looking about for soft spots that could become the targets of his new aggressiveness, and his first choice was Germany. Despite heavy Soviet support Communist East Germany had never been able to legitimize its world position as had the non-Communist Federal Republic. The presence of Berlin, Germany's historical capital, three-fourths of which was maintained as a non Communist enclave right in the middle of East Germany, was a humiliation not just to the German Communists but also for Russia itself.

The occupation of Berlin would of course end if a peace treaty were signed with the German nation as a whole, but the division of Germany between Communist and non-Communist areas had stymied this project for what at the time promised to be an eternity. Khrushchev, who saw the breaking of this impasse over Germany as a chance to reduce America's role on the European continent, threatened to sign a unilateral Treaty of Peace with East Germany, which would withdraw recognition of the Allies' right to occupy Berlin. The threat was made most explicit in a memorandum Khrushchev handed President Kennedy at their meeting in Vienna in June 1961. Backing it up was a huge Soviet military force, whose approximate numbers the Allies knew but about whose modern weaponry they had inadequate data.

One of Penkovsky's greatest contributions lay in providing the United States with intelligence, much of it documentary, that was necessary to evaluate Soviet advanced weapons development. In advance he had compiled a "List of Materials and Documents to be Sent" (see a brief extract of it below). Carried out of the Soviet Union by Greville Wynne, it named documents on a large number of newly developed Soviet weapons systems that he could make available.

Description of Rocket 3Rl	2 pages
Rockets 3R2 and 3R3	2 pages
Rocket 3R7	1 page
Construction of Launching Installation 2P2	6 pages

To quote from a 1964 briefing given by then-Director of Central Intelligence John B. McCone,

> By October 1962, when Colonel Penkovsky was arrested in Moscow, he had supplied us with *over 10,000 pages of Secret and Top Secret documents* [emphasis added] and verbal reports. . . . The bulk of these documents dealt with Soviet military doctrine, strategy, and tactics. In addition, all Soviet tactical missiles, including the surface-to-air missile that shot down the U-2, were described in exhaustive detail in these documents. The documents also included the first two issues of the Top Secret instructions from Soviet Strategic Missile Headquarters to the Intercontinental, Intermediate Range, and Medium Range Ballistic Missile (ICBM, IRBM, and MRBM) field units. These instructions reflected the elementary status of the Soviet ICBM force, and gave data on MRBM

deployment which were critically important for the analysis of the Soviet missile adventure in Cuba.

Our grasp of the implications of Soviet advanced weapons and our intelligence concerning them later became so important that it is easy to forget how different was the situation that President Kennedy faced in 1961. The mere size of the huge Soviet Army gave it considerable flexibility in the level and form of conflict to employ, were it to hazard such a venture. U.S. military forces, on the other hand, were equipped primarily to fight a full-scale *nuclear* war, on the assumption that the United States could not "afford" to fight "limited" wars. If there had to be a war many experts therefore thought it would naturally be a big one.

Regrettably, as of 1959 the U.S. secretary of defense was not sure that we could fight even a "big" conventional war, since he forecast that "the Soviet Union would probably have a 3-1 superiority in intercontinental ballistic missiles by the early sixties." As late as the summer and fall of 1961 the idea of a "missile gap" between the two countries persisted, "with the U.S. Air Force continuing to claim that the Soviets had 600 to 800 ballistic missiles, while the CIA estimated 450, and the U.S. Navy only 200."[2]

Depending on the weight given to various components of our strike forces, including our conventional aircraft, the more extreme estimates of Soviet strength presaged disaster for the Western world. As is so often the case, the bad news made the headlines, whereas America's true relative strength did not. In their quest for sensation certain members of the media therefore relentlessly pressed their cries of doom. To balance the extreme claims of the U.S. Air Force, the CIA was fortunate in having obtained access, through Penkovsky, to one of the best-qualified experts in the Soviet Union. Penkovsky's friendship with Varentsov served us well, for as chief marshal of artillery this old soldier commanded not only the tactical missiles but was also kept fully informed about the longer-range weapons of the Strategic

Missile Command and other Soviet missilery in general.

Varentsov was not just a contact of Penkovsky, he had become a family friend. Not only were Penkovsky and his wife entertained at Varentsov's magnificent *dacha* (a perquisite of power for a man of his exalted rank), but the Varentsovs from time to time stayed overnight at the Penkovskys' modest apartment in Moscow. In this atmosphere of intimacy the chief marshal said one day, "You know, Oleg, with respect to ICBMs, up to now we don't have a damn thing!" In large measure, therefore, the confusion regarding the relative strength of the United States and Soviet forces was resolved by Penkovsky's information, obtained from Varentsov as well as from his studies at the Dzerzhinsky Academy. A summary report, based directly on what Penkovsky had told us, was hand-carried to President Kennedy in mid-1961, which included:

> Khrushchev's basic idea is to be a jump ahead of and to impress
> the leaders of the Western powers—to represent that which he does
> not have or that which he has in insignificant quantities as some-
> thing which he has already in hand. There are tests of one nature
> or another which in many cases are successful, but he is already
> ranting as though this were an accomplished thing. Thus, the
> whole idea of Khrushchev and of the Presidium is to [impress
> Western military leaders] by the launching of an earth satellite, or
> even a man in space. . . . This is to force Western government lead-
> ers and military people to do their planning on the assumption that
> the Soviet Union already has a tremendous military potential, when
> in reality it is only being developed.
>
> Source [Penkovsky] then referred to Khrushchev's threats, and
> recalled that a senior general officer of artillery [Varentsov],
> responsible for one aspect of the Soviet missile program . . . told
> source in early 1961 that "We are only thinking about these things,
> only planning. . . . But in order to get anywhere one has to increase
> production tremendously and to train cadres." The officer stated

further that the Soviets have in their arsenal tactical [short-range] missiles, and [also] missiles that can reach South America, the United States, or Canada, but not accurately.

There are [also] test missiles which are still undergoing further tests and are not on bases. [But] there are not hundreds [as Khrushchev had implied], even in a testing status. . . .

Even now [Penkovsky concluded] it may be possible that somewhere in the Far East . . . there may be some missiles which could reach other continents and detonate with an atomic, even hydrogen, explosion, but such launchings would be completely unplanned, uncontrolled, and certainly not of a mass variety. Of this I am entirely sure, though in two or three years there will be a different picture.

Reports such as this, when added to masses of irrefutable documentary evidence that Penkovsky had photographed, cut the Soviets down to size in President Kennedy's mind. Later one authority wrote that "On Thanksgiving week-end, when the President convened his defense experts for a meeting at Hyannisport, the weight of evidence was plainly against the Air Force, and the [missile gap] issue finally withered away."[3]

A Friend in Need

Penkovsky did not wait for intelligence to come to him. Instead he created his own collection opportunities. One of his inspirations was to write an article for a Soviet Army publication on some aspect of military science, thereby justifying increased access to a wide variety of classified information. His background both as an artillery officer and as a graduate of the Dzerzhinsky Academy qualified him for the job. When Penkovsky mentioned his plan for the article Varentsov immediately offered him the use of an office in his own headquarters.

Having thus acquired access to one of the Soviet Union's two principal missile headquarters, Penkovsky lost no time in exploiting it to the fullest. Outgoing and convivial, Penkovsky soon made the acquaintance of a number of officers in the headquarters, among them a certain Lieutenant Colonel Dolgikh, head of the Secret Section that had custody of all classified files. Penkovsky immediately befriended him—and, as was so often the case, with less-than-pure motives.

As Penkovsky explained his technique in talking to one of his case officers, "I am always doing something for others, and maintain good relations that way. Often I give presents, of course refusing any reimbursement. I also entertain; or, through Varentsov, arrange for favors, such as getting someone a telephone." Dolgikh, the perfect target for such attention, was not hesitant in sharing his troubles with Penkovsky, whom he knew to be a protégé of the illustrious chief marshal. The poor lieutenant colonel, it seemed, was caught in one of those imbroglios so typical of Soviet bureaucracy. He had for some time shared a two-room apartment with a certain Colonel Kuznetsov and the latter's half-blind son. The military administrative authorities had decided to resettle Dolgikh elsewhere, in order to give both rooms to Kuznetsov and his son. Where would the lieutenant colonel live? He was told to address himself to the municipal authorities. Unfortunately, no one had taken into account that at about the same time the municipality had reduced the allocation of lodgings available to military personnel, and no vacancies were available. Dolgikh would soon have no roof over his head.

The situation presented an obvious opportunity for Penkovsky to ingratiate himself with the officer who had custody of some of the Soviet Union's most precious secret files, and he rose enthusiastically to the challenge. Having helped Dolgikh prepare a letter to the city council, he then arranged for Varentsov to sign it personally. Faced with a communication from the chief marshal, the municipality was suddenly very obliging. "And that," Penkovsky smilingly told his case officers during one of his visits to London, "is how I get along with people."

Penkovsky's kindness quickly paid off. "Dolgikh is a great big fellow; he should be a blacksmith rather than the custodian of the Secret Section. I simply told him that I wanted to look up some material because I had to prepare a lecture, and he said, 'By all means, help yourself.'" This new access represented a turning point in the operation. Having by now been furnished and trained to use a Minox camera small enough to fit in his pocket, Penkovsky was thenceforth able to photograph documents rather than copying them by hand. Each visit to the vault at Varentsov's headquarters thus resulted in his obtaining hundreds of pages, rather than the mere handful that had been possible before.

THE BERLIN CHALLENGE

By early 1961 a new crisis had developed between the United States and the Soviet Union, centering around Berlin. Penkovsky's reports were among those that first alerted President Kennedy and his principal advisers to the major effort Khrushchev was planning to make to weaken the Allied hold on the former German capital, then occupied in part by the Western Allies but nonetheless completely surrounded by the Soviet forces in East Germany. To Kennedy a threat to dislodge the West from Berlin was simply the first stage in a longer-range Soviet effort to weaken NATO. In Kennedy's words, "all Europe is at stake in West Berlin."[4]

The first documentary evidence of the Soviet Union's exact intentions as of June 1961 was made available by Penkovsky in a clandestine meeting with an Allied representative in Moscow. Similar contacts continued through July, thus alerting Washington, step by step, to new Soviet maneuvers. The main points, summarized in the first of Penkovsky's clandestinely delivered messages, were as follows:

---

1. The Soviet Union, for the avowed purpose of
undermining the position of the Western Allies in

Germany, has decided to sign a peace treaty with East Germany. It will henceforth be called the German Democratic Republic (of which the German initials will be DDR).

2. Once the peace treaty with DDR had been signed, the Western Allies' access to Berlin will be restricted. A state of combat alert will be declared, DDR troops will block the highway between West Germany and Berlin, and access routes will be patrolled by tanks and aircraft.

3. Troops of both the DDR and Communist Czechoslovakia will be put on a war footing, and those armies will be given limited support by the Soviet armed forces. However, the Soviet plan makes clear, "we would want any clash to be brief and limited in scope if the West should move up tanks and other weapons to seize and consolidate communications with Berlin."

4. Because of restrictions imposed on the Western Allies' access to Berlin, "they will have to negotiate with the DDR, and this is very important."

A separate Soviet comment on the plan read as follows: "While recognizing the risk, we believe there will not be a major war, although there may be a local clash only on German territory, and limited to a small area."

Despite the Soviet Government's confidence in its own invincibility, Penkovsky's advice was that "firmness must be met with firmness. . . . It would be advantageous to announce a major redeployment of Western troops. . . . It is necessary that this be exaggerated, but it is also necessary actually to increase Western strength for a quick, sharp blow at the Soviets." The U.S. response was much as Penkovsky had recommended, for by the end of June the American media reported Pentagon plans to call up National Guard divisions, reinforce U.S. troops in Germany, and resume nuclear testing.[5]

A report from Penkovsky in mid-July was therefore somewhat reassuring: "The firm stand of President Kennedy has created quite a panic in Moscow. Since the Soviets did not expect determined reactions on the part of the Western leaders, the advantage now lies with the West." Partly as a result of this report, on 25 July the president called Khrushchev's bluff in a major speech:

> We cannot and will not permit the Communists to drive us out of Berlin. . . . The fulfillment of our pledge to that city is essential to the morale and security of Western Germany, to the unity of Western Europe, and to the faith of the entire Free World. Soviet strategy has long been aimed, not merely at Berlin, but at dividing and neutralizing all of Europe, forcing us back to our own shores. We must meet our oft-stated pledge to the free peoples of West Berlin, even in the face of force, in order to maintain the confidence of other free peoples.

Kennedy's speech was in large measure made possible by Penkovsky's intelligence on the true state of the Soviet Union's offensive capability, which was weaker than many had supposed. The U.S. policy of firmness paid off, and it was not long before Penkovsky reported that "Khrushchev's tone is now softer. This shows that our [the Allied] governments and leaders have taken the right action. That's the way to treat the dogs!" Penkovsky's analysis proved correct. Although Khrushchev tried to keep the pressure on, his bluster gradually lost its credibility as the Allied side continued to call his bluff. By early 1962 the Berlin Crisis had subsided.

A ONE-MAN WAR

At times Penkovsky seemed to be waging his own one-man war—

against the Soviet Union as a whole, and against Khrushchev in particular. These were, of course, intemperate times, with the leader of
the Communist Party (whom President Kennedy described as filled
with "inner rage") setting the tone. But Penkovsky, in spirit if not in
deed, was an equally sanguinary human being. His continually frustrated ambitions, as well as his craving for a degree of freedom he
could never hope to achieve while living in the Soviet Union, make his
frequent emotional eruptions understandable, regardless of how exaggerated they may seem to those never personally exposed to the bru-
tality of the Stalinist and immediate post-Stalinist eras. During
Penkovsky's trips abroad his CIA and British case officers had come
to know him well, and they accepted his violent proposals with the
equanimity due a genius voicing his every daydream.

Penkovsky took three visits to the West: two to London in
April–May and July–August 1961, and another shortly thereafter to
Paris, all of which encompassed a number of lengthy clandestine
meetings. Penkovsky was always met by the same team of four case
officers (two American and two British), all of the meetings were
audio taped, and most tapes were transcribed in detail. Since it
appeared that he articulated almost any thought that went through his
mind, these transcripts provide ample evidence of the motivation
behind his frenetic activity. Indeed, if there were any difficulty in
defining his personality from the lengthy record of conversations with
him, that difficulty lies in an overabundance rather than a paucity of
material.

During the case officers' early meetings with him Penkovsky's
obsession centered around an elaborate preemptive nuclear strike
against the leadership and principal military installations of the Soviet
Union. This grisly project was to be carried out not from the air by
missiles, but by "saboteurs" on the ground. Leading these saboteurs
was to be none other than Penkovsky himself. As he pointed out, the
strike was to be against Moscow, and who knew that city better than

he? His plans came bubbling forth like unexpected geysers encountered by chance in the wilderness. For discussion purposes some order must be arbitrarily imposed upon them, as follows. During the first London meeting with him in April 1961, as he went over a map of Moscow to show the case officers the location of key military installations, his remarks went somewhat like this:

> The general staff of the Ministry of Defense is located in the Arbat area. . . . This should be blown up with small, two-kiloton bombs. . . . [And then] as a strategic intelligence officer, a graduate of two academies, and having worked for some time in the general staff, I know what the sensitive spots are. I am convinced that my viewpoint is absolutely correct, namely, that in case of a future war, at H-Hour plus two minutes all of the critical targets such as the general staff, the KGB Headquarters on Dzerzhinsky Square, the Central Committee of the Party . . . must be blown up by prepositioned atomic bombs, rather than by means of aircraft bombs. . . . Such weapons would not need to be set within the buildings themselves—there are many neighboring buildings where they can be concealed, because dwellings and stores are adjacent. For example, there is a large *gastronom* [grocery store] next to KGB Headquarters. A small group of saboteurs equipped with such weapons, governed by a time mechanism, should plant them in locations from which all these Headquarters can be destroyed. . . . All Military District Headquarters must also be destroyed. These headquarters can be easily spotted in every major city. All one would need would be one bomb per Military District. This would destroy the mobilizational and organizational directorates which are the backbone of the armed forces [and] reduce the combat strength of the Soviet Army appreciably.

When he was in these demoniac moods Penkovsky's predictions were invariably dire:

We all know the Soviet Union is a dangerous foe who wants to be the first to attack us, and she will do this—when all is prepared . . . some dark night she will do it! . . .

When H-Hour takes place, then you [will have] just two minutes. Everything must be in readiness, by way of mines equivalent to one or two kilotons—they can be put in a little suit-case (this is just my own idea)—a little satchel, and left next to a house . . . and let the whole establishment go up in smoke. Then, when the leaders . . . the general staff and the central directorates . . . tanks, artillery, aviation, anti-aircraft . . . when these are all destroyed, then let's see them pick themselves up! . . .

The best time for the explosion would be between 10 and 11 A.M., because all the command personnel would then be in the buildings. We poor workers begin our day at nine in the morning, but command personnel with late breakfasts, engagements, et cetera, don't arrive until about ten.

A building Penkovsky particularly wanted to see eradicated was KGB Headquarters in the center of Moscow: "It has seven sub-basements. In the seventh, there are chambers where Russians—prominent people, patriots, wise people—are exposed to rats. . . . There is one special room which is completely glazed. Anyone who cannot be broken or who will not say what they want him to say, or who will not sign something, is put in the middle of this room. There are pipes leading into it made of clear plastic, [and] through these, they release dozens of rats which run around [nipping at] the man. Through a microphone they say, "Well, *now* will you tell us with whom you are working?"

As Penkovsky talked his imagination seemed to feed on itself, his description of Soviet horrors became more elaborate, and his voice grew stronger as he spelled them out. There is no record in the meeting transcripts that his handlers challenged the veracity of his statements, nor perhaps was there any reason for any doubt as to his truth-fulness. The intelligence officers with whom he met were themselves all specialists in Soviet matters, and there is no record of incredulity on their part.

A Double Life

Penkovsky's life had been strangely ambivalent for a number of years. Despite his rage against the system in which he was caught, on the surface he continued to live outwardly by its rules until his death and, moreover, seemed proud of his ability to do so. His development of a close relationship with the man who was at first chairman of the KGB and later of the GRU, Ivan Aleksandrovich Serov, and with Serov's family, is an example of Penkovsky's commitment. Once when speaking to his case officers in England, he described his success in this regard as "a cunning, intelligent maneuver." The ground had been prepared by the fact that Chief Marshal "Varentsov is a great friend of Serov. At one time Serov was one of [the chief marshal's] regimental commanders. Then Lavrenty Beria [head of the secret police until he was himself executed in 1953] took him on, and he soon shot to the top."

Later, when Serov was transferred to the GRU, he was undoubtedly a source worth cultivating; not only was he Penkovsky's chief, but his eldest son [was] married to Khrushchev's daughter, Yekaterina. Although Serov embodied the characteristics of the Soviet system that Penkovsky detested most, one case officer claimed that Penkovsky regarded the GRU chief as "simple, kindly old Ivan Aleksandrovich." On at least one occasion, however, Penkovsky's assessment was much less charitable: "Serov is not the most brilliant of men," he said, "he just knows how to interrogate people, imprison them, or shoot them."

This last remark may have come, however, from only one part of Penkovsky. Having immersed myself for some time in his sayings and doings, I cannot but believe that there was another side of Penkovsky that genuinely enjoyed the company of powerful men and the glory their friendship as reflected on himself. If that be so, it was no crime, and even at his most vituperative he would have had to admit that Varentsov and Serov were loyal to him until his last days. After the trouble over the Turkish visit Penkovsky never returned Serov's loyalty, yet the GRU chief was among the men whose friendship Penkovsky most assiduously cultivated—exclusively, or so Penkovsky wanted his case officers to believe, because it was in the interest of his cause to ingratiate himself with those in power. Indeed it was; Penkovsky's strength as a spy was that, after having done so, he had no repugnance about manipulating any of his high-ranking friends for his own purposes. A deeply rooted double nature is the sine qua non of espionage.

Look for a moment at Penkovsky's kindness to the Serov family. Could it have all been a sham? By happenstance Serov's wife and daughter had made arrangements to visit London on the same date as Penkovsky himself, and Serov had asked him to take care of them, ensuring that someone accompanied the ladies on their shopping expeditions and that they had a car at their disposal. The Serovs duly arrived on a special plane sent over to collect the Kirov Ballet Company. Yet, although the chairman had himself sent a cable asking that they be met, the Soviet Embassy had somehow failed to take note of this request, and "on arrival there was no one at the airport, no car, nothing." Penkovsky, who by total coincidence had arrived on another Soviet plane at almost exactly the same hour, therefore found himself in a position to shine gloriously.

With great courtesy he got the two ladies to their hotel, then offered to show them around the city the next day. English-speaking and by now knowing London well, he won their hearts by showing them the sights of the city, buying them a meal at his own expense, and escorting them to a nightclub, where he danced to the rock-and-roll music with the twenty-two-year-old daughter, Svetlana. The Serov ladies were overwhelmed, perhaps in part because he even volunteered to carry back some of their many purchases. It is not surprising that Penkovsky had barely returned to Moscow when Serov called him personally. "You seem to have disappeared," he said. "We want to see you!"

"Comrade General, when should I come?"

"Tomorrow, at six o'clock!"

Penkovsky then reeled off the names of those who lived in the same building as the Serovs—many of the most distinguished Soviet leaders of the time. "All these live at No. 3 Granoskogo Street, to which your obedient servant goes as a guest! Well, I arrived, gave [the chairman] his shirt and all the little things. They laid the table. I was the only guest, but we got on very well." Nonetheless, though his position seemed to be improving, he was still cautious. "Two or three days after I had seen Serov, I was summoned by the deputy chief of the GRU Third Directorate. He said, 'We are thinking of sending you to the United States. You would go to the embassy [with the rank of] counsellor, but your work would be for the GRU.' That is where the conversation stopped. What will come of it, God only knows."

Whatever happened to that plan we do not precisely know. It seems likely, however, that in some way the KGB's suspicions had already been aroused, and that it again interposed an objection. If so, Penkovsky's fate already hung in the balance. However well-connected he might have been, Penkovsky was thus with good reason uncertain of his future and never felt he could relax. The mere fact of being on friendly terms with Varentsov, Serov, and other generals was not enough. He had to keep proving himself over and over; he feared he would not survive otherwise. He was a Russian, after all, and he well knew the portent of his origins. "In Moscow [he told his case officers one day], a real KGB bastard sits in the Central Committee, in the Exit Visa Section, by the name of Colonel Daluda. . . . He decides who will go abroad and who will not. This time he let me go, because it was just a short trip and both the GNTK and the GRU approved. But they would not trust me on a long-term assignment. . . . If it weren't for the affair of my father, I would be recommended for the rank of general, but now this will never happen."

Notwithstanding his discouragement, Penkovsky never flagged; he said on one occasion, "I am very persistent," obviously understating the case. On his three trips abroad, which were of course the only occasions when his case officers could observe his performance first hand, he displayed a capacity for concentration and hard work that evoked wonderment among them. Had his GRU superiors been able to observe him without divining that he was in fact working against rather than for them, they would have been delighted at his performance.

The function of the subordinate GRU organization to which Penkovsky was assigned, the GNTK, was industrial espionage—the collection of information on the West's advanced technologies through a combination of overt and clandestine techniques. Certainly Penkovsky was ideally qualified for this role. In addition to being aggressive at developing contacts, he also had a strong technical bent. Penkovsky had a number of inventions to his credit, from rather diverse military fields. He had patented an "angle-measuring artillery compass" in 1938; he also developed a complicated system for adding explosive charges to antiaircraft barrage balloons that would blow up aircraft bombs on contact (a device that in practice was too expensive to be used). Furthermore, while at the Military-Diplomatic Academy he had written a thesis on an innovative idea for a clandestine communications technique, for which he received a one-thousand-ruble prize.

Penkovsky's technical aptitude shone through most significantly, as far as we were concerned, in his photographic ability. On the basis of only a brief training session conducted in a safe house, his document photography, obtained in Moscow where he had to exercise his new skill under the most difficult and stressful conditions, was close to perfect. To enhance his cover, on the other hand, he was given invaluable assistance by his case officers, who provided stage-managed introductions to various U.S. and European businessmen, a good deal of unclassified but nevertheless significant technical information from various firms, and, on one occasion, detailed instructions on photographing a British airfield. "I received thanks in Moscow for my reporting, especially for all my photographs. They show the new antiaircraft system in England," he later reported.

Unlike Pyotr Popov, Penkovsky was a self-starter. He had not the slightest hesitation about initiating contacts and on one occasion even had to be restrained from making it because he did not properly understand the security problems involved. He could not, for example, grasp why his case officers could not operate as freely in France as they had in England. "But surely France is our country?" he said in bewilderment, as if Western Europe were simply one huge nation of interchangeable jurisdictions.

One of Penkovsky's initiatives, conceived in London following a visit to the grave of Karl Marx, was out of the ordinary, even by his own innovative standards:

> I thought of doing something this morning. I believe I will go
> through with it. . . . When I arrive in Moscow in two or three
> days, I shall write a personal letter to Khrushchev. This will be in
> the form of a report which I will sign. . . . When I visited the grave
> of Karl Marx [at Highgate, in north London], I noticed that the
> monument and the immediate site are in a horrible state of deterio-
> ration. Old withered flowers, broken bottles, and cans used as
> flower containers are scattered about. The great monument to the
> founder of Communism is completely neglected by everyone here. I
> have taken photographs, and they clearly show the extent of the
> neglect. . . . I will make suggestions as to how the situation could
> be improved. This should win me good marks from both

> Khrushchev, and also Serov, through whom the letter will be for-
> warded. I'll simply write this as a good Communist who feels it is
> his duty to call attention to a disgraceful situation.

As he had predicted, Penkovsky's initiative was well received: "I submitted a letter, which went to the Central Committee, who then told
the embassy to allocate money for the payment of the caretaker of the
cemetery to clear up the grave, and instructed people working in the
embassy to check on this more often. [In Moscow] they can now see
that I am alert to both military and political problems!" One can
imagine his wry smile at this remark.

Thus, mixed with the long periods of frustration and unhappiness,
some up-beat moments did occur. Penkovsky never wavered in his
determination to quit the Soviet Union "in one or two years," yet
there were times when his future as an army officer looked almost
bright. It depended, he said, on the all-enveloping authority of the
Central Committee of the Communist Party. He still believed that he
was under serious consideration for a high-ranking post in
Washington, and no negative statements had recently been made concerning him by the Neighbors. Best of all, Serov wanted to promote
him to general.

Few people have ever worked harder for a promotion. While in
London on his second visit Penkovsky requested that his case officers
procure a bottle of fine cognac, exactly sixty years old, to be given to
Chief Marshal Varentsov on his sixtieth birthday. A suitable brandy
was accordingly procured, but Penkovsky knew that it was *appearance,* not flavor or bouquet, that would count, and unfortunately the
bottle did not bear a sufficiently decorative label; he therefore requested that a more impressive one be somehow concocted. A substitute
label was promised, but here the historical record fails; one may
assume that something more appropriate was obtained, though the
request may have exceeded even the considerable capabilities of

Penkovsky's case officers. By definition secret intelligence agencies have little to do with matters akin to the supremely public arts of marketing and salesmanship.

With or without the new label, when Penkovsky nonetheless returned to Moscow, he was delighted to find that the chief marshal of artillery had come personally to meet him at the railroad station:

> I had brought him the cognac, a lighter shaped like a missile, and a cigarette case. . . . He kissed me on both cheeks, [then] told me to be sure to come on 16 September at 1600 hours, together with my entire family, to his dacha. He said that the minister of defense, Malinovsky, would be there, and Viktor Churayev, one of Khrushchev's right-hand men. . . .
>
> Malinovsky brought a magnum of champagne, and also a big cake shaped like a horn of plenty. Churayev brought a large wooden eagle on a stand. Varentsov said that "my boy" (me) had really tried to do everything from his heart. I felt like telling him that there were really *five* boys involved, me and my four case officers! . . .When we sat down, Varentsov told me to do the honors, so I opened our cognac. It turned out to be out of this world. The minister wanted to drink nothing but that cognac. I made it go around for everyone three times. . . . They began to feel tipsy after the first round because the minister offered a toast to Varentsov and everyone drank bottoms up.

In the midst of all this high living Penkovsky was a study in self-contradiction. He glowed as he talked about his social triumphs, obviously having enjoyed them at the moment. Yet the frustration of not fulfilling his soaring ambition could not but embitter him, and his resentment could only be enhanced because he believed, with reason, that he was intellectually superior to the prominent men before whom he had to kowtow.

In conversation with his case officers Penkovsky's disgust with the system emerged most clearly. He was so well-placed within the web of military and political gossip that he never lacked scurrilous stories to tell about the great figures of the regime. Yet he had more than just gossip to offer; many of his tales accurately reflected the class-ridden corruption that existed at all levels of the Communist "classless society." Take Anya Martynova, for example. An intermittent paramour of Penkovsky's, she was the director of a government-run store set aside for general officers. As he described her, Martynova was always "loaded" with diamonds because the high-ranking customers who enjoyed her fervent favors after hours were also generous benefactors. "What a spider's nest it is!" Penkovsky exclaimed. "A high moral standard is supposedly demanded of everyone—people are persecuted, beaten, thrown out of the Party for corruption—but this is how the bastards carry on themselves!"

Behind such denunciations, some of which might perhaps be dismissed as the product of mere intemperance and frustrated ambition, there lurked much larger difficulties, most of which centered around Khrushchev, whose arrogance revolted Penkovsky. The power of this fat, ugly, yet hyperactive man hung over Russia like a swirling tempest from 1958 to 1964, and he exercised an unseen but nevertheless intuitional influence right down to the level of everyday intelligence activities.

PENKOVSKY VERSUS KHRUSHCHEV

During the early part of World War II Penkovsky served in the Ukraine, the huge southwestern area which during the nineteenth century was to Russia proper what the American Far West was to the eastern United States. Penkovsky, though a military officer, was also a *politrabotnik* (usually translated into English as "political commissar") and, in that capacity, ultimately responsible to Khrushchev, who as the political boss of the Ukraine outranked the marshals and generals, even on the battlefield.

Once Khrushchev had elbowed his way to supremacy at the national level, this bumptious little man was verbosely sanctimonious about Stalin's misdeeds, though in the end he did not set a much better example than the evil old dictator himself. A story that dates from 1942 has to do with a certain General Podlas, one of the many thousands of officers who had been executed or imprisoned by Stalin and then rehabilitated when the German Army launched its invasion. Podlas commanded the Russian forces defending the major city of Kharkhov but, finding himself faced by superior enemy forces, was on the point of ordering an orderly retreat when suddenly Khrushchev arrived. The fat little commissar was enraged when he learned of Podlas's plan to withdraw. He reminded the general of his arrest in 1940, then screamed: "You got away with murder at that time, Comrade General. Keep in mind that this time it will not be so easy. . . . I myself, with my own hands, will blow out your brains! I'll shoot you to death like the lowest dog! I order you—continue the offensive!"[6] Podlas, of course, had no choice and, as a result of following Khrushchev's orders, his army was wiped out. Clearly foreseeing his own doom, Podlas then shot himself.

Penkovsky also certainly knew of his friend Serov's long association with Khrushchev. When Khrushchev was boss of the Ukraine, Serov commanded the NKVD in that region. In the latter capacity one of Serov's duties was to deport unwanted populations; when it came time to deal with the Crimean Tartars, however, he discovered that this group included an unusual proportion of old women, young children, and others either too ill to move or simply unfit for work. Serov's solution was a simple one: he had them drenched in gasoline and burned alive. Much later, when Serov had perhaps mellowed, his loyalty was no longer sufficiently unswerving to suit Khrushchev. The general therefore was removed as chairman of the KGB and transferred to the GRU. From that job he always did his best to defend

Penkovsky, but in the end when the showdown eventually came Serov proved no match for the secret police that he himself had once commanded.

The Mind and the Heart

It is tempting to account for Penkovsky's extraordinary performance by assuming that he was jealous of the power and wealth of men more publicly successful than he. But the facts speak otherwise. Though Penkovsky liked money he was not a greedy man. His extravagant expenditures went mostly for gifts—such as the sixty-year-old cognac—that were satisfying to him mainly in that they successfully promoted his access to intelligence. Though he constantly took enormous personal risks and worked diligently, he was only truly extravagant when he submitted to unusual temptation.

Once he was on the U.S. clandestine payroll, neither he nor his family lived any better or worse than they had before. In 1961 his salary from the CIA was fixed at one thousand dollars per month, which at the time was about the same amount paid to a medium-level U.S. civil servant sitting safely behind a desk in Washington. That sum did not even go directly to him, but instead into an escrow account in the United States. According to his contract, drawn up by a CIA lawyer, it was to be used "at such time as his services lose their value [and] he requests the U.S. and British governments to give him and [his] family political asylum and citizenship in one of these countries."

Penkovsky did admit that under certain circumstances "money melts away from me." Yet, when one examines that admission, it doesn't stand up. He was generous to a fault, but spent little on himself. With the naivete of one who has never had much money, what by American standards was a modest sum seemed a considerable amount to him. How little did he know of the extravagant sums expended on less-rewarding intelligence activities! In truth, having grown up in a society that provided few material rewards or incentives, Penkovsky had little understanding of the value of money. In his dealings with prostitutes in London, for example, he was at one and the same time sentimental but rather stingy. After a night on the town with Wynne and some of his friends, "they picked up a twenty-three-year-old girl for me . . . a good girl. She has a pretty name. I spent two hours with her at her apartment. Everything was modest, but good." Asked how much she charged, he replied, "Wynne said fifteen pounds, and I paid her through him." Two days later Penkovsky was still talking about her. "You know, she really fell for me. Two hours was really very short. She was really a bit surprised that I left so soon. She lives pretty well. She has this apartment—I don't have such a nice one! I asked her, 'Why don't you get married?'" It could never have occurred to Penkovsky that the English prostitute's standards of material wealth were so much higher than his that she was probably unable to grasp his question.

Cautious though he had been with the girl, preferring to pay her through his English friend, in more important instances Penkovsky was far from miserly. At the end of what turned out to be his last visit to London, his emotional parting from his case officers was the occasion for one of his most memorable *beaux gestes*. He said, "It is almost two years since I started gathering material for you, but I have now been in active [face-to-face] cooperation with you for three months. I am most grateful and satisfied with my collaboration with all of you, and wish to thank my American and British leaders (meaning the Queen and President Kennedy) for all the help and encouragement given me." Then, focusing on the hard work of the case officers, he continued, "I would like to ask my leaders to thank you for the great work you have carried out.[7] Let them take from my own personal means [the money in his U.S. escrow account established by the CIA] enough to give each of you 1,000 pounds; to the photographer and wireless operator 250 pounds each; while all the technical secretaries, the workers, translators, etc., should receive 100 pounds each." At long last Penkovsky felt he had been admitted to the "new world" of which he had for so long wanted to be a part; this grand gesture was his acknowledgment of the fact. He was also saying that, though Mother Russia had rejected him by frustrating his ambition for advancement, he had found another imposing maternal figure to replace her.

By the luck of history a woman reigned in England at the time and helped fulfill his need. Penkovsky had not originally offered his services to England, but it is plain that he did not strongly distinguish between one English-speaking country and another. His indiscreet approaches to Britons, Americans, and even a Canadian imply that he, much like Popov, had reacted to them all as if they were citizens of the same nation. The Americans had at first been slow in responding. Then when Wynne, an Englishman, finally agreed to transmit a message for him, Penkovsky at the last moment added a handwritten addressee, "Queen of Great Britain, Elizabeth II." Interestingly, he addressed her as "My dear Queen" and President Kennedy as "My dear President." The equivalent of the "dear" salutation is not pro forma in Russian as it is in English, and it is only used with those whom the writer does literally cherish.

In transferring his loyalty to new governments Penkovsky had crossed at least as high an emotional threshold as does the man who physically abandons his country. Indeed, in Penkovsky's case it could be argued that the trauma threshold was even higher, because he faced an additional risk from trying to combat Russia from within rather than working against it after having taken the precaution of going into exile. Yet we must not be overly logical. It is doubtful that Penkovsky ever weighed the pros and cons of what he was about to do in advance. His actions were dictated by the sort of overpowering impulses that cancel out careful calculation. He really had no plan, no map to guide him in this new world of mind and spirit, whose psychic boundaries and contours, emotional mountains and valleys, were an unknown wilderness. Once his effort was launched, however, he was like one of the early seafarers: his eyes were constantly searching the horizon for some new coast, some new venture.

William Bradford, an early historian of Plymouth Colony, summed up the Pilgrims' plight by asking, "What could now sustain them but God and His Grace?"[8] In Penkovsky's case there was no God in whom he believed and on whom he could depend. Instead he sought reassurance in being accepted by ranking members of the British and American governments. Within the context of our workaday democracy, insistence on such contacts may seem a bit absurd, but psychologically Penkovsky was an exile living in constant uncertainty—even about his physical safety. Within the society he had secretly renounced he had for years been comforted by kind words from people at the top—Serov, Varentsov, and Malinovsky, to name a few—but their encouragement no longer had real meaning. He needed to refurnish his world with authority figures whom he could genuinely respect and look to for reassurance. Not being a mystic, he wanted to see them in the flesh.

During his second trip to London he brought up a matter that had probably concerned him for some time. When he and his four case officers came together for one of their regular meetings, he announced, "I would like to meet for five or ten minutes one of the important members of your government. I would like to have you introduce me, and I would like personally to describe [to him] your important and difficult work with me." His case officers, hardened intelligence professionals strangely insensitive to his yearning for reassurance, were slow to react. Five days later the record shows that they were still asking him to explain his desire to "meet an important person." Penkovsky volunteered,

I have prepared an answer for your question. I expected your question. . . . I consider that I am not just some sort of an agent. No, I am your citizen. I am your soldier. . . . I did not come to you to do *little* things. If I had not had sufficient clandestine capabilities . . . I, as an intelligence officer and one with higher education, would not have dared to presume to come to you with such definite demands. But I consider that I have such unusual and special capabilities for agent work that I shall be able to help my Queen and my President as would a combat soldier. If the governments I now serve value this effort of mine, which was carried out under conditions of exceptional danger and of definite self-sacrifice . . . if there be real value in what I have already done . . . and if you believe that I am not just a run-of-the-mill person . . . then attention from above would be an appropriate recognition of my work. You already love me in your way—as a friend, as a comrade. You believe in me. But the other leaders are not here—those who direct things, I mean. May God grant that you can convey to them all my wishes and potential!

Because two of the three series of meetings abroad took place in England, trying to satisfy Penkovsky's demand for recognition at a high level fell principally on the British. Finally, therefore, an appropriate Englishman identified only as "Sir Richard" was produced, purportedly as a direct representative of Lord Mountbatten, chief of the defense general staff and cousin of the Queen. Penkovsky seemed momentarily flattered: "My dear sir [he said in English], I am most grateful to the Lord and yourself for this attention. It is to me an indication of your recognition of me. I wish to assure the Lord and yourself that very little time will pass before you will recognize me still further, and even have an affection for me. . . . I would like to express the great desire which I have carried in my soul. . . . I even thought about this in Moscow . . . to swear my fealty to my Queen, Elizabeth II, and to the president of the United States, Mr. Kennedy." In the end, however, "Sir Richard" was not quite enough. "Although circumstances do not permit this now," Penkovsky announced even before the meeting was over, "I hope that in the future I shall be blessed . . . personally by the Queen."

By the twenty-ninth meeting of that series the harassed case officers were still trying to make clear to Penkovsky that "it is not possible, under secure circumstances, to arrange a meeting with a member of the Royal Family. The Queen is always accompanied by her entourage." So, as he left London after his long series of consultations with the British and American case officers, Penkovsky still cherished the hope that he might eventually "kiss the Queen's hand," but for the time being he settled for a lesser symbol. "I am taking home a pound note," he said solemnly and in all seriousness, "because it carries a portrait of Her Majesty."

Within the CIA I have heard some people—though not those who had actually worked with him—describe Penkovsky as vain. That is the last thing he was. Consider this brief quote from him, made after his meeting with "Sir Richard":

> **Penkovsky:** I did not lose my presence of mind in front of him, did I? I told him everything that was innermost, but tell me as friends for my own future reference—did I do all right?
> **Case officer:** Yes, on my word of honor.
> **P:** As regards the form—the actual presentation of everything—was it correct?
> **C.O.:** Very proper, well done.

This exchange speaks volumes about Penkovsky's insecurity, which could only increase as he came more and more to live in two antagonistic worlds: one that he understood all too well and hated, and another that he comprehended imperfectly but dearly loved. Increasingly, as his secret life fulfilled his need for an abstract blend of love and loyalty, his ties to fellow Russians became progressively artificial. In Moscow, of course, he had innumerable friends and acquaintances, people who not only filled his time but unwittingly provided the raw material for many of his reports. Yet George Kisevalter, the bilingual American, had an interesting observation: "The most glaring facet of Oleg's character to me, as a person who grew up in Russia, is his lack of a really significant human relationship. With the exception of Marshal Varentsov, who was like a father to him, he never referred to any Soviet male as a friend. . . . He had *no* close friend. This is in considerable contrast to all the other defectors I have met."[9] Penkovsky was a loner in more ways than one. He knew how to use people, how to extend favors that would benefit him in return, but he had no genuine friend for friendship's sake.

While he was in the West, however, it is not surprising that Penkovsky was frequently lonely. Once out of Russia the only people he knew were Wynne and his case officers. They, however, were severely restricted in where they could see him. "Although a good soldier, he could not understand why we could not eat dinner with him in some suburb of Paris," one case officer observed. Another CIA man records this incident: "He was once observed strolling along late at night up the Champs Elysées. As he passed a sidewalk café he walked directly in front of us, obviously noticed us, then very reluctantly continued on his way. He badly wanted to *belong* and appeared to live for the moment when operational meetings began and he took stage center among his admiring friends." Friends? Yes they were, and their very uniqueness was no doubt why he never let them down.

Mercifully, the case officers *could* satisfy one of Penkovsky's entreaties without much trouble. Penkovsky had requested the uniforms of general officers in both the British and American armies. He did not seem displeased when told that, not being himself a general, he would have to settle for the appropriate dress of both nationalities in the rank of full colonel. During the second London visit, one night the two uniforms were produced at the safe house and, with great care, he initially put on the British uniform. He was then photographed, first while wearing the visored cap, then without it. Next came the U.S. uniform, and again photographs. "He was obviously delighted," says a report of that meeting, "and on his own initiative he repeated the oath of allegiance to both countries."

LAST DAYS ON THE "FRONT LINES"

When Penkovsky left Paris in October 1961 his last visit to the West had ended. He had no inkling, however, that the end was near. Ten days before his departure he wrote the director of central intelligence, Allen Dulles, telling why he was returning home: "Despite my great desire to be with you even now, I feel that for another year or two I must continue in the General Staff of the USSR, in order to reveal all the villainous plans and plottings of our common enemy. In other words, I consider, as your soldier, that my place during these troubled times is on the *front line*."

When meeting Penkovsky a few days later, the case officers commented that he was "at the highest egotistical pitch ever noted." They quoted him as saying, "I am only one person but I am strong!" The last meeting ended after Penkovsky had, in traditional Russian style, "kissed and hugged each officer in turn" and all present had "sat down for a moment of silence." Penkovsky was never sent abroad again. There were already tell-tale signs that the KGB was suspicious of him, the most significant of which was that organization's refusal to allow the powerful Serov ever again to employ his friend outside the borders of the USSR. Under such circumstances security precautions had to be redoubled. The most important of the new measures adopted was the assignment to Moscow of a charming Englishwoman named Janet, who will always live in intelligence history.

The wife of a British Embassy officer recently assigned to Moscow, Janet served loyally on what truly was the "front line." She had been selected and specially trained for her unusual intelligence assignment, and had even met Penkovsky and outlined the details of their Moscow meetings during one of his trips abroad. As a woman it was thought she would be less subject to KGB surveillance than a man; she had a cool head and, even better, a lovely baby. Referred to by those who were directing these meetings from behind the scenes as the "baby-carriage lady," Janet regularly took the child to a park where she and Penkovsky could encounter each other as if by chance. They never chatted for long; and the object of their meetings was simply to allow him to pass film cassettes of documents he had photographed, which he could do easily by simply dropping them into the carriage as he leaned over it briefly as if to admire the child.

The Moscow aspect of the operation had in fact always been the dominant one, because it was there that Penkovsky turned over the bulk of his intelligence. From the time of the Paris meeting, however, there was mounting fear that his compulsive desire to film every valuable thing he could get his hands on would sooner or later lead to disaster. The case officers themselves felt helpless and frustrated because Penkovsky would not listen to their warnings. Yet they knew he was over-confident, particularly when operating in his own capital. The following descriptions, based on CIA reports made in May 1961, give some sense of Penkovsky's style during this period

Wynne flew in to Moscow on the afternoon of Saturday, 27 May. He had with him a parcel of umbrellas and three suitcases, one of which contained purchases made on behalf of Penkovsky. Of the items Penkovsky had ordered, everything had been loaded on the plane with the exception of a large chandelier, which simply couldn't be packed. On arrival at the Moscow airport, Wynne was at first dismayed at seeing no sign of Penkovsky, then with some relief caught sight of him hurrying across the tarmac. Arriving at the customs shed, Penkovsky flourished an official pass that got Wynne through Customs and Immigration without any formalities and in record time. Outside the terminal building there waited an old, broken-down black car, and at the wheel was an elderly and equally decrepit driver who appeared to be a friend of Penkovsky. The car was already heavily laden with parcels that Wynne surmised might be the product of black-market dealings.

Rather than heading directly into Moscow they drove out to the countryside. Along the way Penkovsky, without comment, passed Wynne three packages, which the Briton accepted just as wordlessly. At last they pulled up in front of a wooden shack. Here the driver's wife appeared, and helped unload Penkovsky's parcels, while Wynne presumably kept a tight grip on the three packages Penkovsky had previously given him.

This sequence of events is not explained in the record, and is cited here merely as evidence that Penkovsky sometimes behaved in aberrant fashion instead of trying, as he should have, to remain inconspicuous. After this mysterious transaction had been completed the disreputable taxi reversed direction and chugged back into town, finally drawing up in front of the Metropole Hotel located in the center of Moscow. On the way Penkovsky pointed out the sights, while Wynne handed over cartons of cigarettes and some special hair lotion. (While in London Penkovsky had poured Old Spice aftershave lotion on his scalp, which caused his hair to turn purple. It was hoped that the lotion would correct this anomaly.)

Upon entering the Metropole, Penkovsky again produced his official identity card, plus a letter from the GNTK directing that Wynne be given special consideration, including a car that would be available to him throughout his stay. As soon as he had settled in, Wynne set off for a prearranged meeting with a Moscow-based case officer, to whom he handed over the three packages of intelligence just received from Penkovsky. During such meetings no conversation took place, all communication being in sign-language or by written notes that were subsequently destroyed.

The three packages turned out to contain over fifteen hundred pages of photographed documents of the highest importance. From where these particular pictures were obtained is not clear from the record, but Penkovsky seems always to have carried his Minox camera with him, and his photography was sometimes done on the spur of the moment. In a letter passed to Janet in late December 1961, for example, Penkovsky wrote that, while in the office of Colonel Vladimir Mikhaylovich Buzinov, an aide to Varentsov, "I saw on his desk [certain documents the chief marshal had written] on missile questions. Buzinov gave them to me to read and went out for a few minutes, leaving me with all his secret papers. I quickly photographed these. (For reliability, I took them twice.) This is *extremely* important material, which was reported to the Supreme War Council in the presence of Khrushchev and other members of the Government." In the same letter Penkovsky promised to photograph a 420-page manual, and asked whether another manual, 216 pages of training in the use of nuclear weapons, would be of interest.

The professionals handling the case understandably reacted ambivalently to such exploits, but they were helpless to do anything about them. When, during one of his visits to London, Penkovsky was criticized for taking undue risks, he replied that "while in the UK I will listen to your advice, but in Moscow I call the plays." In Washington a desk officer wrote that the incident in Buzinov's office "is but the latest and most dramatic illustration of a problem which has been troubling everyone connected with the case for some time. . . . [But] our frequent admonitions to be careful, to think first and foremost of his own security, to meet Janet less often, etc., etc.—taken in the context of our simultaneous requests to retake p. 18 of this, pp. 11–13–15 of that, and pp. 1–420 of the other—are of a 'stop it, I love it' nature, and have clearly been interpreted by Penkovsky in this vein."

Because the meetings with Janet were at Penkovsky's initiative, whereas she simply visited the park in accordance with a pattern normal for a mother giving her child regular outings, the case officers had little control of how often those contacts took place. "Janet is in the

park with her son, who is by now about two and a half years old,"
reads one operational report from Moscow.

> Penkovsky appears on the scene, and then proceeds down one of
> the streets leading from the area, selecting a different one each
> time. Janet follows after him, occasionally with some trouble per-
> suading her young son to leave the piles of snow in the park.
>
> Janet dresses in such a manner that she does not feel she is
> conspicuous as a foreigner. Penkovsky meanwhile enters one of the
> doorways along the side street and stands behind the stair well, so
> that he can observe anyone coming down the stairs or through the
> door. Janet enters, and is with him about ten seconds, sometimes
> more. She passes anything for Penkovsky in a package of Russian
> cigarettes, and he passes material to her in a package of English
> cigarettes. They always exchange a comment or two about such
> things as family health, etc.

Hyperactive as ever, during one eleven-week period Penkovsky had
shown up ten times for such meetings. "He revels in what he is
doing," wrote one case officer, "is determined to be the best of his
kind ever (not appreciating that he has probably already achieved this
status), and sees in his relationship with Janet the symbolization of his
relationship with the Allies." More and more the case officers felt out
of touch with Penkovsky's personal situation because their communication with him was now largely through Janet, and thus indirect.
Had he overstepped the bounds of the possible? Was he under suspicion? The KGB's capabilities in Moscow were so all-encompassing
that even intensive surveillance on the officers' part would be hard to
detect.

In January 1962 a joint U.S.–British business group visited the
USSR, and Penkovsky was their escort officer. From an initial debriefing of a member of that group it was learned that he was clearly in
charge, talkative, well dressed, his health appeared good, and he gave

no hint of anxiety. Then abruptly the picture worsened. From a later debriefing it was learned that Penkovsky had approached one member of the U.S.–British group to ask that a message be delivered to someone in England (whose name does not appear in the record). When duly delivered the message was that Janet was now under KGB surveillance. Yet, though the noose was tightening rapidly, Penkovsky did not substantially modify his behavior.

Another member of the same delegation, a Russian-speaking American, had been observing him with interest and later commented on his "apparent duality." In the presence of other Soviets he was the typical officious party-liner. At a banquet in Leningrad, for example, he got up and delivered a militant speech about peace and friendship, Communist-style, that could well have served as a model for any Soviet after-dinner speaker. On the other hand, when alone with delegation members he would offer unusually candid remarks that clearly breached Soviet official policy.

Communication with him, which for some time had been episodic, now became more and more difficult and infrequent. In March 1962 Janet happened to meet Penkovsky at a diplomatic reception. She noticed that he circulated very little at first, but when eventually the two of them happened to be near each other he asked in a low voice, "You must be feeling rather tired; why don't you rest for a few minutes in the hostess's bedroom?" Two or three minutes after she had followed his suggestion she overheard him saying to the hostess, "What a lovely flat! Would you show me around?" Then, as he was led into the bedroom, he apologized for disturbing a lady, winked at Janet and, as he turned to leave, casually exposed a cigarette pack in his hand clasped behind his back. It was visible only to Janet, and with great presence of mind she grabbed it. The cigarette pack contained several letters, and eleven rolls of Minox film. One of the letters warned Janet that she was being followed whenever she went out, another talked of his own problems. Things were going badly, he wrote. "The KGB are rummaging around concerning my father. . . . My command [the GRU] considers these fears meaningless and they are defending me from all these conjectures of the Neighbors."

The trip to the United States which the GRU had scheduled for him was now definitively canceled by a direct order from the KGB delivered to Serov. Ironically, though it was too late, Penkovsky now wanted to leave. A letter, found in the record in Washington and which somehow got to the United States, read: "I am sick and tired of all this. I feel that I do not have sufficient strength. . . . I very much want to come to you. Even today I would leave everything and would depart together with my family from this parasitic world. What should be done for the future? I request your advice." A few days later another said, "My wife has given birth to a second daughter. Try to send a coat, dress, suit, and baby shoes, all this for a girl one year old." The letter concluded, "I shake your hand very firmly. Always your friend."

In July Greville Wynne visited Moscow to conduct the last prolonged contact any of our representatives was to have with Penkovsky. He did not meet Wynne at the aircraft as he had on previous occasions, but did meet him inside the terminal and escorted him through customs. When they reached Wynne's hotel room Penkovsky broke down and started sobbing. He looked tired and nervous, and for the first time admitted the hitherto inadmissible: he was frightened. Later in the day he asked Wynne to get him a small-caliber pistol. He slept every night, he said, with a knife in his bed, ready to commit suicide if the police came.

Scheduled to meet Wynne for dinner the next evening, he was late in getting to the rendezvous point because he had spent so much time reconnoitering the area to check for surveillance. Upon finally meeting the two men then walked through a park to a small restaurant. Over dinner Penkovsky asked Wynne to inform his friends that, whatever happened, he wanted to carry on working until September. After that, although he would obviously prefer to take his family with him, he was prepared to leave Russia on his own.

The next day was a difficult one for both men. "At about 8:45 P.M.," Wynne said later, "I took a taxi near the American Club, and arrived at the Pekin Restaurant at about 8:50 P.M." He walked around a block, testing for surveillance, and having detected none headed back toward the Pekin. On the way he passed a doorway in which two men were standing. Pretending not to notice them he continued on, stopping to look into shop windows along the way, but noticed that the men had left the doorway and appeared to be following him. Then he saw Penkovsky walking toward the restaurant, and he did the same, timing his movements so that he and Penkovsky met in the crowded doorway. As they met Penkovsky made a furtive gesture, indicating that they must not make contact. Penkovsky tried to get into the restaurant, but finding it full—a routine experience in Moscow—he left and walked out again, quickly rounding the corner.

Wynne made a pretence of trying to get a seat, but eventually also gave up. On exiting the restaurant he saw the same two surveillants lurking in the shadows on the opposite side of the road. He did not look round; the best thing, he decided, would be to go back to his hotel and hope Penkovsky would contact him. Suddenly the whole world was hostile. Having hailed a taxi he found that the driver did not want to accept him. In mid-argument, however, he caught sight of Penkovsky making his way down what was apparently a private drive leading into a small housing complex. As the taxi departed Wynne followed him. When they finally made contact in the shadows of the apartment buildings Penkovsky whispered quickly, "You are being followed. . . . I'll see you in the morning," and vanished in the shadows.

Wynne turned but found that the surveillants had also disappeared, probably into the housing estate. When with intentional bravado he changed direction and went looking for them, they seemed startled and retreated quickly in the face of his advance.

IN THIS IS MY STRENGTH

In late August 1962 the CIA received from Penkovsky more document photography, as well as his last communication. As the work of a man who knew that he and perhaps his family faced imminent arrest, the message is striking in its calm acceptance of reality. He does not entirely give up hope for the future, but accepts probable torture, trial, and death as the hard facts that they are. Even when confronting martyrdom he wrote his case officers a long, remarkably restrained letter (excerpted here):

> *My Dear Friends,*
>
> *It will soon be a year since our last meeting. I am very lonely for you, and at the present time still do not know when we are fated to see each other.*
>
> *I and all the members of my family are in good health. I am in good spirits and capable of working.*
>
> *I have already become used to the fact that periodically I note surveillance and control over me. The "Neighbors" continue to study me. For some reason they have latched on to me. . . . I confuse and lose myself in guesses and suppositions.*
>
> *In drawing conclusions, I want to emphasize that I am not disappointed in my life or my work. I am full of strength and desire to continue our important work. This is the goal of life. And if I succeed in contributing my little bricks to our great Cause, then there can be no greater satisfaction.*
>
> *It is not advisable to make a decision now to cease photography. It is necessary to continue this work until they take away my official identity document.*
>
> *If they remove me from the GNTK, I will make a last attempt to remain in the Army by appealing to [Defense Minister] Malinovsky, Serov, and Varentsov. . . . If this doesn't help, I will not remain in Moscow. I ask you to understand this and to sanction these actions and decisions of mine.*

There was a dreamlike quality to what happened during the next two months, because no one in Washington or London wanted to admit that this uniquely successful intelligence operation was drawing to a close. Nor was Penkovsky much more realistic. As a well-informed Russian who knew better than any foreigner the relentless intensity of KGB investigators, he nonetheless continued to labor at his mission. "I have found two very good dead drops," he announced in his final letter. "I do not want to visit the dead drop sites for detailed study while I am being watched. I will send the descriptions later."

He worried also about his future and that of his family, while always trying to come up with positive answers to his own questions. He asked for an objective reevaluation of the value of the intelligence he had produced for which, he believed quite rightly, he had not been adequately compensated. (By August 1962 the balance in his U.S. escrow account amounted to some forty thousand dollars after two years of incredibly valuable work. Though a substantial sum, it was modest indeed in proportion to the results he had achieved.) Never losing hope, he asked that the CIA consider a lump sum payment once he left Russia "because I want to acquire right away my own active enterprise. . . . I am very interested and concerned by the question of what will remain after me for the people near and dear to me." He continued, "I assure you at once that if my request is turned down the quality of my work and all my enthusiasm will not diminish by one grain. . . . Believe me, in this is my strength."

Ironically, with U.S. and British ability to contact Penkovsky reduced to a minimum, the need for his assistance suddenly increased. U.S.–Soviet relations had reached a new crisis, this time in the Caribbean. On 23 October 1962 Washington sent an "eyes only" cable to the chief in London, asking British assistance in getting a message to Penkovsky. The previous day, said the message, "President Kennedy announced that we have firm evidence that the Soviet Union is equipping Cuba with means of offensive warfare, including surface-to-surface missiles. . . . Since the situation is changing rapidly, we do not want to give you specific questions which might be out of date by the time you receive this communication. We want to say only that all concrete information about the military and diplomatic moves being planned or undertaken by the Soviet Union is of vital importance." Unfortunately, the message was too late. Penkovsky was under arrest.

THE TRIAL

We do not know with certainty how Penkovsky was finally unmasked by the KGB and, since the present study is principally concerned with the personality and motivation of espionage agents, here is not the place for the endless counter-intelligence analysis and speculation that is easily possible.[10] Instead, the relevant facts are as follows: Our first indication that Penkovsky might be under arrest was the detention by KGB plainclothesmen of an American intelligence officer while he was unloading a dead drop in Moscow on 2 November 1962. This unfortunate event was quickly followed by the arrest of the indomitable Greville Wynne by the Hungarian police in Budapest on 4 November; they turned Wynne over (obviously by prearrangement) to the Soviets. Penkovsky and Wynne were tried in Moscow simultaneously, before the Military Collegium of the Supreme Court of the USSR, during a trial that lasted from 7 to 11 May 1963.

A British diplomat who attended the trial later recounted his memories of it, in these words:

> The court room was stiflingly hot. . . . Soviet cameramen (their Western colleagues were not permitted to bring in cameras) were much in evidence. Every dramatic moment was heralded by the withering glare of klieg lights and a sudden excited whirring of cine-cameras that almost drowned the words which followed.
>
> The presiding judge did not give the impression of being a strong personality. . . . His occasional questions to witnesses and defendants did not appear either pertinent or intelligent. He did

not take a single note throughout the proceedings but appeared to have some kind of script on which he ticked off the prosecutor's questions. . . .

The prosecutor put question after question in a tired and rasping monotone. He rarely raised his voice, showed no emotion and did not attempt to arouse any. His strategy was simply an exhaustive interrogation of the defendant [but he] showed little resource. On the rare occasions when Penkovsky failed to give the expected answer and did not respond to prompting, [the prosecutor] appeared nonplussed. . . .

Penkovsky's counsel was a nondescript man of unimpressive voice and presence who appeared cowed by the hopelessness and pointlessness of his role. . . . [His final speech] was badly delivered as though he knew the case was lost, and he began by more or less apologizing for defending Penkovsky at all.

Penkovsky, on the contrary, gave evidence confidently, almost eagerly. He showed no sign of emotion or even awareness of the inevitable outcome. He was self-assured, fluent, and appeared to derive satisfaction from the competence of his performance. He did not give the impression of having been brain-washed or drugged, for there was nothing mechanical in his answers.

At the same time, his mental state was not entirely normal; he appeared to be acting under some sort of stimulus. Perhaps [this was no] more than the excitement and relief of performing in the limelight after months of intensive and lonely rehearsal.

The British Embassy record of the trial indicates that, although Penkovsky "attributed his crimes to his moral defects—drunkenness, vanity, desire for an easy life," he also was contentious in regard to certain points that reflected on his character. "The prosecution's [intent]," the British report added, "was to play down Penkovsky's importance in every way, and to do so they produced only two insignificant Soviet nationals as witnesses." One of them, the driver of the taxi that Penkovsky had used to pick Wynne up at the airport, alluded to Penkovsky's having had a number of affairs, and said that he was "mainly interested in food, drink, and women."

The other witness, a certain Finkelstein not further identified, was slightly more significant, if one can believe his own account of himself as offered from the witness stand. He claimed to have been introduced to Penkovsky about 1952, and although they never became intimate friends, he had noted in Penkovsky certain "negative traits—vanity, arrogance, self-love." At one point the prosecutor broke in with the following demand: "Tell me, witness, tell me about the evening in the restaurant in which instead of glasses, wine was drunk from a woman's shoe."

"This happened at Poplavok Restaurant," Finkelstein replied. "One of the women was Galya, whom Penkovsky was attracted to. . . . Somebody said that out of respect for a woman we should drink from her slipper. We approved of this, laughing, and Penkovsky actually drank wine from Galya's shoe."

The presiding judge then asked, "The slipper was taken from her foot?"

Finkelstein replied, "It was." He later mentioned that Penkovsky "earned more money than the rest of us," though he did not explicitly cite that fact as grounds for jealousy. There then followed more serious testimony. An expert in handwriting testified that certain notes (apparently made from classified Soviet documents) were in Penkovsky's handwriting, and other official papers had been copied on his typewriter. Then came Expert Chemist Kuznetsova, who answered questions about two sheets of clean white paper taken from a secret place in Penkovsky's apartment. "The two sheets," she said, "contain a special chemical substance on the surface which makes it possible to use them . . . for writing an invisible text." Next a man identified as Expert Naumov testified that the radios and ciphers found in Penkovsky's possession were appropriate for communications

with "the American spy center at Frankfurt-on-Main [which] trans-
mitted one-way broadcasts of enciphered radiotelegrams in Morse."
Culminating the testimony, as recorded in the official Soviet record,
was Penkovsky's admission that he absented himself from his duties
with the GNTK delegation on more than one occasion, because "I
was at meetings with intelligence officers. . . . I received an assignment
to set up and activate contacts with persons who could provide information of a military, economic, and political nature." It was also mentioned that he "became personally acquainted with the English
woman intelligence officer Chisholm, Janet-Anne, wife of the second
secretary of the British Embassy in Moscow, Roderick Chisholm,"
who was also an intelligence operative. "One might say," the record
adds, with an unexpectedly light touch, "that spying was the family
profession."

Other parts of the Soviet record are also not without humor—
though it was probably unintended—as, for example, its treatment of
British-American relations. "The American intelligence officers evidently decided to 'cuckold' their British partners and to arrange a
meeting with Penkovsky unbeknownst to the latter. [At this meeting
the Americans] expressed regret that Penkovsky was working with the
British; they promised him mountains of gold if only he would come
to America." (It is self-evident that a human being will confess to anything if subjected to sufficient duress, particularly if his captors also
have his wife and children in their hands.) Within the severe limits
imposed on him, Penkovsky comported himself well. A British barris-
ter who came to Moscow to assist Wynne but who was never allowed
to participate in the defense, agreed that Penkovsky "gave no sign of
having been brainwashed. Indeed, Penkovsky's whole bearing, which
was one of fortitude coupled with remarkable intellect, impressed me
greatly. Nevertheless, the whole thing appeared to me as an admirably
rehearsed play."

"On the final day," says the British Embassy record, "the court was packed suffocatingly with a Roman circus audience, thumbs pointed firmly down. Wynne's sentence, to eight years of 'deprivation of liberty' was greeted with applause, but insistent calls of 'not enough' made the details of the sentence inaudible even to his own counsel."

Penkovsky was sentenced to be shot. When this announcement was made it was "greeted with delighted applause and the courtroom benches creaked under the weight of stout, grinning matrons who clambered onto them in their eagerness to catch a glimpse of Penkovsky's reaction."

In Sum

Those Soviets who were great figures in Penkovsky's time have long since passed from the scene. Khrushchev, who was forced to resign all his offices in 1964, became a "nonperson" ignored by press and public; he is now dead. General of the Army Serov, head of the GRU who, according to a subsequent KGB defector, "backed Penkovsky to the hilt," was demoted three grades and sent to the provinces as deputy commander of the Volga Military District. After Khrushchev fell Serov was expelled from the Communist Party and retired. Chief Marshal of Artillery Varentsov was promptly expelled from the Supreme Soviet and died not long afterward.

What of Col. Charles Peeke, the American whom Penkovsky called his "first good friend" and to whom he might have offered his services in 1958 had Peeke still been in Turkey? In May 1963, when it was feared that Peeke's name might surface in the forthcoming trial, Washington decided that he should be briefed on how to reply to queries from the press. One of the CIA's overseas stations contacted him, then cabled the following report: "He unaware Penkovsky arrest and trial, and has only vague recollection of him." *Sic transit gloria mundi.* Whatever glory there may be for spies, it is likely to be brief.

3
Yuri Nosenko
A Refugee in Hell

A MEETING IN GENEVA

Geneva, beautiful Geneva, beside a lake shimmering in the early morning sunlight. It was June 1962, and KGB captain Yuri Ivanovich Nosenko had received an assignment that was to mark the turning point of his life. He had been sent off to Geneva as the watchdog accompanying a Soviet delegation to one of the many international organizations that regularly met in Switzerland. Having never been outside the USSR before, Nosenko was dazzled by the glamour of the lovely lakeside city.

In Soviet terms Nosenko was reasonably sophisticated, for he did not come from a run-of-the-mill family. Quite the contrary. Born in 1927, he was part of the so-called "golden youth" raised at the top of the Soviet Union's social pyramid. His father had been minister of shipbuilding and a member of the nation's supreme governing body, the Central Committee of the Communist Party. So eminent was the minister that upon his death a bronze plaque commemorating him had been affixed on the Kremlin wall. Given this family background it is not surprising that Yuri eventually obtained an appointment as an officer in the KGB, a position sufficient in itself to make him a working member of the Soviet elite. Moreover, his first assignment was in the American Embassy section of that organization, a prestigious appointment and a clear indication of good connections. Nosenko continued to be promoted, each step forward serving as an entrée into something even better. Eventually transferred to the section that monitored tourists, he quickly became the drinking companion of his chief, a general. The barrier of rank between the two was erased by Nosenko's father's eminence; with the benefit of such patronage he was soon promoted to deputy section chief, a position that qualified him for the widely sought privilege of foreign travel. His first opportunity to travel was a visit to Geneva, where we pick up his story. Nosenko had no particular intellectual distinction and little sense of responsibility, and his only major fault was one shared by many of his contemporaries—a weakness for liquor.

Having visited a number of bars the previous evening, Nosenko awoke on his first morning in Geneva and did not feel quite up to par as he lifted the shades of his hotel bedroom window. The seductions of the idyllic city had been irresistible, and happily his duties as a KGB escort officer were undemanding. Taking advantage of the fact that the traveling delegation members for whom he was responsible could not watch their watchdog, he had split off from them soon after the evening meal. From then on, in this town full of attractive nightspots and seductive women, drink had followed drink, and suddenly he was back in his hotel bedroom with a smiling presence at his side—his last memory until he regained consciousness the next morning.

Once fully awake he could remember little more than inviting the prostitute back to his hotel. Suddenly alert, however, he quickly searched the pockets of his suit and of one thing he could be certain— the smiling girl had absconded with most of his expense allowance, some two hundred and fifty dollars worth of Swiss francs. Not only would he have nothing to live on during his stay, but before his departure he would have to submit a fully documented accounting of what he had spent. The KGB penalties for mishandling funds were severe, so there was no way of replacing the lost money by simply appealing to one of his colleagues permanently stationed in Switzerland. Such an admission, implying that the watchdog himself needed watching, could then and there have ended his career. What to do?

As Pyotr Popov and many others like him had done, Yuri saw an answer: he would present himself to the American Croesus. As a typical example of the aptly named golden generation, Nosenko enjoyed having money and was unencumbered by qualms about whence it came, so no problem of principle stood in his way. Moreover, as a KGB officer he knew that Russian defectors were reputed to have been well treated by the Americans who gave them asylum, particularly if the Russians provided useful information.

Providentially, Yuri remembered seeing, right in the heart of Geneva, a magnetic center of temptation: the large and conspicuous U.S. Consulate General building. That was where he would go! In making this decision, however, he could hardly have been expected to imagine that from the time he made contact with an American, his life would never again be the same. Nor could he have foreseen that events would turn out as tragically as they did.

Nosenko's quest for help seems at first to have proceeded with the simplicity of a childhood dream. Naively presenting himself to a U.S. consular official, he was asked to answer only a few questions before being assured that help would be forthcoming. All he had to do was make himself available the next evening at a nearby apartment, the address of which he was given. He immediately agreed, having no way of knowing that this rendezvous would turn out to be the most fateful few hours of his life.

Nosenko did, however, become increasingly apprehensive during the night, and grew even more nervous as he made his way through unfamiliar streets to the meeting place the next evening. As a KGB man himself he knew that this appointment in a private apartment building smacked of clandestine activity; he presumed, therefore, that he would not be meeting regular consular officials, but rather intelligence operatives. He was uncomfortably aware that a number of KGB people were stationed permanently in Geneva, people whose responsibilities were to keep an eye on the many Russians working in the city's international organizations. He had no idea how thoroughly they covered Geneva, but as he neared his destination he worried more and more about the perils of keeping his appointment.

Another less tangible concern weighed on his mind. Except for his brief contact with an American consular official the previous morning, he had never before met anyone from the United States. What were they like, these Americans? Themselves so rich, would they understand his problem? As he usually did when under strain, Nosenko decided to have a drink. That first one soon led to several more. Nervously, to be sure he was not being followed, as he left each bar he checked for familiar faces loitering in the neighborhood. This procedure was repeated several times: bar, drink, look around for anyone he might recognize or suspect as a KGB surveillant, then circle the block again. Try as he might he could not shake the concern that he himself might be under surveillance by fellow Russians, and he believed his salvation lay in making contact with the Americans as quickly as possible. But first, another drink!

When he finally arrived somewhat behind schedule at the meeting, he was met by a CIA team headed by a vigorous young intelligence officer named Tenant Bagley, very much an American in appearance and not a Russian speaker, accompanied by the bilingual George Kisevalter, Popov and Penkovsky's old friend, who would serve as interpreter. Both had been quickly dispatched from different parts of the world especially for the rendezvous.

The American case officers received their visitor with apparent cordiality and, not knowing how much Nosenko had already had to drink, offered him another. He accepted, and throughout the meeting never seemed to have thought of turning down whatever was proffered. As he said to me many years later, "I must tell you honestly, John . . . I was snookered."

"You mean you were drunk?" I asked.

"Yes, I was drunk, very drunk."

QUESTIONS OF BONA FIDES

June 1962 was a bad time for Russian defectors. Within the CIA an aberrant personality named James Jesus Angleton had for some time reigned over the counterintelligence (CI) staff at the agency's headquarters near Washington. The combination of Angleton's undisciplined mind, perfervid imagination, and willingness to see Communist-sponsored subversives and spies almost anywhere and everywhere led to wild theorizing about the extent of the subversive threat to the United States—not just in Angleton's mind but in those of many of his associates and disciples as well.

Bagley had greatly underestimated what was to be the CI staff chief's reaction to Nosenko's offer to provide intelligence to the CIA team in Geneva in return for an amount of money equaling that stolen by the Swiss prostitute. It was nothing more than a childish proposal made by an immature young Russian, but to Angleton's acolytes it had all the earmarks of a malevolent effort to establish a working relationship with the CIA to "penetrate" the agency. Such subtle, sinister arrangements did indeed occasionally constitute a problem, but in this case the CI staff should have been mature enough to see Nosenko's initiative for what it truly was: a plea for help from a very unsophisticated young man. Had the agency team come equipped with easily portable polygraph equipment manned by a competent operator, some of the doubts might have been quickly resolved. Instead, all that was available was the collective intuition of Bagley and Kisevalter.

In his discussions with me many years later Nosenko confessed to having made things worse by bragging a good deal and overstating his accomplishments—not excessively, perhaps, by the standards of drunken social chitchat, but in this inquisitorial context it was enough for his exaggerations to be used against him later. The situation may have been worsened by the fact that a CIA tape recorder was on hand at all the meetings, though it functioned only sporadically. Its actual performance was of less significance, however, than the fact that later on, when transcripts were supposed to have been made, it wasn't used systematically. Most of what were thought to be "transcripts" turned out not to have been made from the recordings at all; instead, they were notes written on the basis of Kisevalter's memory of what Nosenko had said. (The making of the "transcripts" necessarily devolved onto Kisevalter because Bagley, though he had studied Russian, was not able to conduct interviews in that language.) Nonetheless, these inaccurate "transcripts" became enshrined in the CIA's files as the official record and were later used as "documentary evidence" that Nosenko lied during this and later meetings. As a result Nosenko was discounted as a potentially valuable source of intelligence—and eventually became a victim of Angleton's ever-deepening suspicions. To cite one example of inaccurate transcription, in reciting his personal background Nosenko mentioned that he had attended a naval preparatory school bearing the name of a Soviet military hero, General Frunze. This accurate detail of his education unfortunately went into the CIA record in distorted form, as a claim that he had graduated from the Soviet Union's version of West Point, the Frunze Military Academy. A trivial detail, certainly, but useful to Bagley and others who later busily searched for proof of what they thought was this naive young man's duplicity.

Superficially the first meeting ended on a cordial note, and no wonder. Nosenko had identified several agents of the KGB who were serving as penetrations of U.S. installations abroad. His potentially most important information, however, concerned a threat to the security of the American Embassy in Moscow in the form of micro-phones buried in the building by the KGB. Unfortunately, he could not identify the offices in which the listening devices were located, he did not know whether they were concealed in walls, floors, or ceilings, and he had no idea how many such devices had been implanted. Since this information was not only imprecise but embarrassing, the U.S. State Department used Nosenko's lack of precision in support of an unwritten but nonetheless widespread bureaucratic rule: bad news should be ignored whenever possible. It was therefore not until eight-een months later, in January 1964, when Nosenko returned to Geneva with exact details regarding fifty-two listening devices planted in every important part of the U.S. Embassy in Moscow, including the ambassador's office, that this major audio penetration was at last investigated and confirmed.

In any case, however, by the end of the June 1962 meetings and even before the confirmation of the audio installations, Bagley felt with good reason that his mission to Geneva had been successful. On 11 June 1962 he sent a cable to the CIA in Washington in which he gave assurance that Nosenko had "conclusively proven his bona fides. He has provided information of importance [and is] completely coop-erative."

SUSPICIONS

Before proceeding the reader must be warned: the case of Yuri Nosenko is as complex as it is outrageous, and thus may strain both one's patience and one's nerves. Yet it has a great deal to tell us about the realities and dilemmas of the intelligence craft. Unfortunately for him, three sets of circumstances combined to bring disaster upon Nosenko: the tense state of Soviet-American relations, the increasing-ly paranoid attitude of James Angleton, and, ultimately, the assassi-nation of John F. Kennedy all contributed to casting suspicion that this man who had approached the CIA in seeming good faith in June

1962 and later defected to the United States in 1964 was a Soviet plant with a mission to deceive the United States.

Nosenko's story is thus totally different from the first two presented here—Pyotr Popov's and Oleg Penkovsky's—because those two men were accepted as genuine and never suspected of working against the United States. Moreover, Yuri Nosenko was himself quite a different personality than they. In particular he possessed little of that gift for dissembling that had allowed the others to survive while pretending loyalty to the Soviet Union for a considerable period of time during and following their clandestine defections. Nosenko was an uncomplicated man, and when we finally met I noted that though he spoke English reasonably well, he rarely employed abstractions—even such simple ones as "good" and "evil." Years of solitary confinement (more on that later) seemed to have shrunk his mental and spiritual horizons, and all he asked for in life was a minimal level of decency.

Another major difference distinguished Nosenko from our first two cases: he had never really desired to be a spy. Quite the contrary. The valuable information he provided when he first arrived in Western Europe was meant only to accredit him as a useful person to whom we Americans would be inclined to give money. Once hooked, his long-term goal was quite simple: to cut his ties with the Soviet Union and resettle in the free world as soon as possible. Thus when he visited Geneva a second time in January 1964, he came prepared to stay in the West; at that point he formally defected and requested asylum in the United States.

NEGATIVISM IN WASHINGTON

Let us turn our attention to the atmosphere at CIA headquarters at the time Nosenko first appeared in Geneva in June 1962. Two factors that neither Bagley nor Kisevalter had taken into account in their Geneva assessment of Nosenko and their plans for continuing CIA contact with him were the suspicions of James Angleton (which hung like angry clouds over anything and everything having to do with the CIA's Soviet operations), and the naivete of many of Angleton's most senior colleagues. In particular, one very senior officer regarded Bagley's conclusions concerning Nosenko with utter disdain. Let us look for a moment at the prevailing influence of Angleton as chief of the CI staff.

James Angleton was the man who incautiously confided secrets to the Soviet agent, Kim Philby, but a few additional words on Jim may be helpful at this point. When I first met him in Rome in 1948, Angleton was a man of considerable charm. Part of his youth had been spent in Italy, after which he attended an excellent boarding school in England. Later, during and after World War II, he served in the Office of Strategic Services and its successors, first the Central Intelligence Group and later the CIA. As America's espionage chief in Rome after the end of hostilities Angleton gained firsthand experience of the Communists' bold effort to seize power there. His subsequent deep suspicions of their activities anywhere in the world were understandably heightened by that experience.

Having finally left Europe to serve in the agency in Washington, Angleton quickly established a reputation as an intellectual, with an infinitely detailed grasp of Communist efforts at subversion. His tales of Soviet iniquity, replete with allusions to Russians whose names meant nothing to most of his senior colleagues, were accepted unquestioningly because no one had any basis for challenging his daunting authority. It was generally conceded, on the other hand, that Angleton was disorganized to the point that the in box on his desk was a bottomless pit from which little emerged without help from others.

Angleton's most influential years were the two decades during which he headed the CIA's CI staff. The CI organization, redolent with mystery, handled the complex task of identifying spies (primarily from the Soviet Union and its satellites suspected of working against the United States or its allies) with varying degrees of success. Being chief of this organization was an exacting and difficult job that deserved the best leadership the CIA could provide. If Angleton ever met that criterion, however, he certainly could no longer do so by the late 1950s. The carefully cultivated mystique certainly existed, but the man did not. Perhaps because of his legendary thirst, Angleton's muddled mind by then had become a grab bag of haphazard minutiae, much of it totally irrelevant to whatever subject was under discussion.

In 1976, when we were both retired, I found myself back at the CIA, having been recalled specifically to investigate the Nosenko case. During the active phase of this case Angleton had played an important role in persuading most of his colleagues and superiors that Nosenko was an "agent of disinformation" dispatched by the KGB precisely to confuse the U.S. government. His was a challenging and controversial proposition and Angleton knew that I disagreed with him on it, yet when I invited him to visit me in my temporary office at agency headquarters to discuss it, he was thoroughly cooperative.

Beginning at one o'clock in the afternoon I interviewed Angleton for more than four hours, carefully recording everything he said. Unhappily, when his words were transcribed the next day resulting in some fifty double-spaced pages, I was in for a shock: for the first time I realized how disorganized his thoughts and even much of his speech had become. He did not finish many of his sentences, and few of them had much to do with what we were supposed to be discussing. In all honesty I must say that had we had our discussion much earlier, even then I would not have been persuaded by his "disinformation" thesis in regard to Nosenko. Why so much detail on Angleton? Because he, more than anyone else, influenced the atmosphere in which Nosenko was judged at the time of his initial approach in June 1962 and defection in January 1964.

Angleton's intellectual structure, disorderly to begin with, had deteriorated further by 1961 under the influence of a former KGB

major named Anatoliy Mikhailovich Golitsyn. When Golitsyn defected in that year Angleton quickly adopted him as a source and adviser,
even though a CIA psychiatrist had diagnosed the Russian as "paranoid." This serious psychological abnormality was, however, quickly
brushed aside, perhaps for no better reason than that the "shrinks"
were not taken seriously by many CIA executives. Nevertheless,
Golitsyn was well received by Angleton and had a seminal influence
on many people in the agency.

Let us pause for a moment to discuss the intellectual and emotional orientation of this unusual Russian. To begin with, Golitsyn's
feelings regarding Nosenko, who defected after Golitsyn did, were
anything but impartial. Golitsyn believed firmly that Nosenko had
been dispatched by the KGB with the specific mission of either dis-
crediting or actually assassinating him. Centering around his knowledge of the KGB, Golitsyn also depicted an evil, ubiquitous force
aimed at the destruction of the United States and its Western Allies. At
the core of this threat was the schism between the Soviet Union and
Communist China, which Golitsyn saw merely as a trick devised by
the KGB to confuse the West. I still recollect, with both amazement
and regret, that Angleton himself also embraced this fanciful idea
without reservation. Another of Golitsyn's primary themes was that
the KGB, to shield itself against his own revelations, would launch a
counterattack by dispatching spurious defectors to the United States
whose specific mission upon arrival would be to pass "disinformation" designed to discredit Golitsyn himself. Had this idea been
accepted by others as completely as it was by Angleton then one man,
and one man alone—Golitsyn—might well have become the U.S. government's primary adviser on Soviet matters.

Whatever the skepticism elsewhere within the CIA—and it grew
as time went on—Angleton himself accepted the idea of a Soviet plot
to discredit Golitsyn. It was only natural, therefore, that Angleton
quickly rejected the positive assessment of Nosenko sent by Bagley

from Geneva. As Angleton later told me, "We got the first message from [Bagley] . . . and we had a big meeting here on Saturday morning. He thought he had the biggest fish of his life. I mean, he really did. And everything I heard from him was in direct contrast to what we had heard from [Golitsyn]."

When Bagley reported in to headquarters after his June 1962 meetings with Nosenko, Angleton set about changing the younger man's mind by trotting out the writings and debriefings of Golitsyn, which had by now become the "Mosaic Law" of the CI staff. Angleton's prestige caused Bagley to reverse course and accept all these "teachings" at face value. Furthermore, at Angleton's insistence, for several years whatever Nosenko said was submitted for final judgment by Golitsyn (though he was already professionally diagnosed as paranoid). The result of Angleton's acceptance of Golitsyn's theses was the contamination of the hitherto salubrious intellectual climate of many sections of the CIA, as we were inundated by what many of us called "sick think." Consider one example of such perverse thought, which I later used in testimony before a Congressional committee in September 1978: "It was concluded that when [a Soviet] said, 'Yes, Nosenko is telling the truth,' that statement cast a [spurious] reflection on [the very person who made it]. That was taken as pretty clear evidence that [the Soviet] himself was under KGB control. Otherwise, [the Soviet] would not testify to Nosenko's truthfulness."

As a result of his having appeared on the scene just as the institutional paranoia of both the CI staff and the Soviet division reached its peak, Nosenko was to receive treatment at the hands of the CIA that was almost from the beginning based on a presumption of guilt. To the day of his death Jim Angleton insisted that Nosenko had been "dispatched" by the KGB to deceive us; and, having concocted that legend himself, he was certainly not prepared to abandon it. Nor could the legend be refuted by others, since everything having to do with counterintelligence was shrouded in such great mystery.

As to the CI staff itself, the cadre of personnel was a tightly knit group, unified by a complex myth system and so fiercely loyal to their leader that objective self-criticism was virtually impossible. Moreover, the staff's investigations and analyses were so lengthy and abstruse that the few officials above Angleton in the bureaucratic hierarchy had neither the background nor the time to read and analyze the justification for his views regarding Nosenko's duplicity.

THE KENNEDY ASSASSINATION

It was not only within the CIA that events had gone wrong for Nosenko. Our entire nation faced similar problems: 1962 was the year of the Cuban Missile Crisis, and unbounded distrust of the Soviets was perhaps understandably the fashion of the time. In Washington the climate of suspicion in both the CI staff and the Soviet Bloc (SB) division of the CIA had more than kept pace with popular sentiment, spurred on, of course, by the dizzy theorizing of James Angleton.

A major national tragedy then took place in November 1963, the assassination of President Kennedy. Nosenko was in Russia at the time, but because he had worked on the case of Lee Harvey Oswald in an earlier KGB assignment (when the latter was in the Soviet Union), Nosenko quickly became entangled in the investigation of the president's death. "We will bury you!" Nikita Khrushchev had declared in one of his intemperate outbursts, and many Americans and Europeans took his threat literally.[1] The painful memory of that statement made it easy to believe that America's leader had been cut down by a demonic Soviet plot, and the imaginations of many sober-minded men were carried away. It was certainly helpful when Secretary of State Dean Rusk, a member of the Warren Commission (which had investigated the president's death), rendered the common-sense verdict in June 1964 that, "I have seen no evidence that would indicate to me that the Soviet Union considered that it had any interest in the removal of President Kennedy." Nevertheless, as if all that was evil in the world began in Moscow, other Americans remained convinced of Soviet guilt. Among them, of course, was James Angleton.

The convoluted reasoning behind Angleton's suspicion that Nosenko was connected somehow to the assassination of the president—an opinion not founded on any valid evidence whatsoever—can be divided into three acts, all of them pure myth but nonetheless accepted by countless men of rank and stature. The first conceived of Oswald being trained as an assassin by the KGB during his residence in the Soviet Union (1959–63); the second had the young American being dispatched to the United States with the explicit mission of shooting the president; the denouement credits the Soviets with taking steps to exculpate themselves by sending a duplicitous emissary to the United States to proclaim Russian innocence in the affair.

The villain in the last part of this remarkable tale was Yuri Ivanovich Nosenko. Why? No clear or logical reason exists. He fell under suspicion, in fact, because—coincidentally—at the time of his reappearance in Geneva in January 1964, by which date he had made up his mind to defect to the West, Angleton and the CI staff were looking for a culprit. What sort of culprit, and what evidence proves that such a person even existed? The answers to these questions lay in the fertile imaginations of Angleton and a few acolytes in his staff and certain senior members of the SB division, whose collective "intuition"—for indeed it was nothing more substantial than their hunch—led them to conclude that the Soviets would send an emissary, masking as a defector, to mislead us as to the (presumed) direct Soviet role in the president's assassination. For no better reason than that Nosenko was both a Russian and a captain in the KGB who was familiar with Lee Harvey Oswald's stay in the USSR, the CI staff fixated on this young officer as the person who fitted an imaginative scenario of their own invention. They claimed that though this man posed as a defector seeking freedom in the West, he had been dispatched to absolve the Soviets of any involvement in Kennedy's death. From start to finish this conclusion was a matter of bureaucratic convenience, not the product of logic backed by facts.

That Nosenko's actions should be so interpreted can only be understood if one realizes that the agency's CI staff was by now dedicated to a *Cause,* with a capital "c." Much of the research involved to support the theory was carefully conducted and valid, but in other instances the staff's procedures were more like those of the medieval Inquisition than of an empirically based inquiry. In that respect the inquiry's point of departure was the assumption of guilt, regardless of the lack of any proof. For better or for worse, a healthy dose of suspicion is often at the heart of espionage, and may indeed (up to a point) be an essential element of the profession. Suspicion must always be balanced by wisdom, however, and in Nosenko's case that balance was not achieved. Speaking for myself and with nearly a quarter-century's experience in the CIA behind me, when it fell to me to review this affair I had never previously seen such fanatical devotion as that displayed by the perpetrators of the Oswald myth and the consequent incarceration of Yuri Nosenko.

NOSENKO'S RETURN TO GENEVA

Nosenko, of course, knew nothing of the unhealthy climate operating within the CIA, and by the time he returned to Geneva on his second KGB assignment in January 1964 he had already decided never to return home. To establish his claim as a political refugee from the Soviet Union he brought with him the details of the whereabouts of listening devices in the U.S. Embassy in Moscow, as well as a number of documents of considerable interest to U.S. authorities, including the identifications of several hundred KGB officers and spies (the latter both Russian and non-Russian in nationality), which he hoped would ensure a cordial welcome. A cordial welcome he did receive, since he made it clear that he feared some form of Soviet reprisal if he remained more than a few days in Western Europe. He was quickly brought to the United States.

Once in Washington he was at first treated reasonably well, but the cordiality of his hosts was a carefully orchestrated facade. Angleton had by now convinced the management of the SB division that Nosenko was an "agent of disinformation" dispatched by the KGB to mislead the United States. However friendly his CIA officers might have seemed in their dealings with Nosenko, they were duty-bound to think of him as an enemy. Though at first he was allowed some outings in and around Washington, for the most part he was confined for questioning.

Bagley led the team charged with Nosenko's interrogation, though he was no longer assisted by Kisevalter but rather by a different fluent Russian speaker. At Angleton's insistence Golitsyn himself, the original accuser, was also made part of Bagley's interrogation team. Although he did not personally question Nosenko, Angleton was given complete access to the records of all of Nosenko's debriefings, including the tapes themselves, and he helped formulate questions to be asked by other team members. Most Soviet intelligence defectors tended to dislike and quite often systematically denigrated each other, and Golitsyn was certainly at the head of his class in that respect. Nosenko suffered accordingly.

One of the ironies of the way Nosenko was handled is that the issue of Lee Harvey Oswald's relations with the KGB, which should have been uppermost in the minds of those debriefing him, was forgotten early on. The emphasis shifted to the effort to incriminate Nosenko as a clandestine Soviet envoy sent to deceive the United States. Having accepted a priori that such was the case, Nosenko's accusers then discounted not only his testimony regarding Oswald (which only tangentially bore on the shooting of the president), but also everything else he had to say. In due course, for example, CIA interrogators spent hours trying to wring from him a confession that his name was not Nosenko.

Thus, during the four years spent trying to unravel the question of whether Nosenko was a genuine defector or actually a Soviet agent dispatched to deceive the Americans, Lee Harvey Oswald was all but forgotten by the CIA. The agency's attention was refocused on the president's assassination only when, in 1978, a Congressional investigation forced it to address seriously the question of whether the Soviets might have been behind the tragedy in Dallas.[2] In fairness to the agency, even had his veracity not been challenged, what Nosenko had to say about Oswald could hardly have generated much interest.

By the time he first heard of this strange American, Nosenko was a KGB officer involved in monitoring foreign tourists in the Soviet Union. In that capacity he was surprised one day to receive word that a U.S. citizen named Oswald wanted to defect and settle in the Soviet Union. To Soviet officials a request by a young American without cultural or ethnic ties to their country seemed preposterous; Nosenko's direct superior lost no time in turning it down. Since they expected that to be the end of the matter, for the time being the young American was forgotten.

It was not the end of the affair, however. Oswald, a bizarre personality in his own right, eventually reclaimed the KGB's attention by slashing his wrists. A genuine suicide attempt, or just an attention-getter? No one will ever know. Two Soviet psychiatrists, after examining him, limited themselves to one masterly understatement: the American was "mentally unstable." While in a hospital recovering from the damage he had inflicted on himself, Oswald then threatened to attempt suicide again if not allowed to remain in the Soviet Union. This time he was successful in making his case. He could remain, the authorities decided, though he could not receive citizenship. Thereafter shipped off to Minsk to work in a radio factory, Oswald was subject to periodic surveillance, his telephone was tapped, and his mail was intercepted, but he was not otherwise interfered with. In 1963, however, having married a young Russian woman, he and his wife left the Soviet Union without difficulty. According to Nosenko the Soviet authorities were only too glad to be rid of him.

Though virtually every other statement Nosenko made was actively disputed over the next four years, he was never subjected to any "hard interrogation" concerning possible Soviet complicity in the presidential assassination. In fact, his knowledge about the Oswald case was so slight that little more than is mentioned here was obtained when he was originally interrogated, very competently, by the Federal Bureau of Investigation (FBI). CIA interrogators paid little attention to Oswald in part owing to the fact that, in the thrall of Golitsyn, they had other fish to fry. For certain reasons (which will be explained later) they felt that Nosenko might hold the key to a "monster plot" masterminded by the KGB, a plot that in some ill-defined way was designed to "defeat" the United States.

Paranoia? In respect to the Nosenko case, yes. But one must keep in mind that, particularly during this era, the Soviet Union, while undeniably an active competitor for world power, didn't hesitate to employ any methods it safely could. If paranoiacs arose in the American ranks, a great many more operated on the Soviet side, and they were highly active. Consider, for example, a favorite form of Soviet propaganda called "disinformation." In its most sophisticated form disinformation included funneling false information through persons masquerading as supporters of the United States or one of her allies, when in fact such persons were Soviet agents intent on misleading our government or our people. Disinformation might, for example, involve reports that greatly underestimated Soviet military potential, thus leaving our side overconfident. Alternatively, it could involve the exaggeration of Soviet military potential in order to discourage us. Politically the technique could also be used to either build up or destroy the reputations of important government figures, both in the United States and abroad.

We in the Western democracies deplored such techniques, of course. Yet from time to time we could not help being their victim. Disinformation simply involves the perversion of facts to serve a political purpose, and though Golitsyn did so without evil intent, he achieved precisely this kind of distortion. If a lesson can be drawn from the experiences of the relatively modest young Russian named Nosenko, on the other hand, it is that the Soviet Union was not the only place in the world where an almost Orwellian perversion of the truth could take place.

DEFECTOR HANDLING

A few words about the handling of defectors are needed in order to establish a contrast with Nosenko's experience. Many defectors feared that they would eventually be killed by the very people to whom they surrendered themselves. From such experiences my colleagues and I had learned how traumatic defection can be for those seeking help, and traditionally the CIA always treated defectors not only correctly but also kindly. Yet the treatment meted out to Nosenko was the exact opposite. It is useful to study the contrast, and the reasons behind it.

Once he arrived in Washington in February 1964, and was face to face with American skeptics, Nosenko's honesty was his undoing. He did not, like Golitsyn and many other defectors, embroider or even distort what he knew in order to excite his interrogators' interest and thus enhance his own value in their eyes. Had Nosenko come bearing intelligence indicating a real possibility of Soviet involvement in the death of President Kennedy, almost certainly he would have been spared the four most miserable years of his life. As an important witness giving valuable testimony regarding a crime to which the nation was deeply sensitive, he would then have been taken out of the hands of the CIA and placed in the custody of competent and reasonable men at the FBI. Such a fate, however, was not to be his, for it is clear that essentially Nosenko's message was a negative one. His knowledge of Oswald was not sufficient grounds for the FBI to claim priority in regard to his custody.

When he left the Soviet Union in 1964 and headed for Geneva, again as a watchdog, Nosenko's intention was never to return. He, of course, had no way of knowing that in the meantime Angleton and Bagley had built up an elaborate case against him. In dealing with him the CI staff's senior officers, led by Angleton, had agreed that those in contact with him must avoid "tipping the agency's hand." An initial pretense of cordiality was therefore maintained for almost two months after Nosenko's arrival. The best way to project this atmosphere of duplicity adequately is through a quotation from the record:

> **Nosenko:** The only thing I want to know is . . . what should I expect in the future?
> **Bagley:** The following awaits. As I presented [your case to my superiors], you wanted to come to the United States to have some job, some chance for a future life which gives you some security, and if possible the opportunity to work in this field which you know. Is that correct?
> **N:** Absolutely.
> **B:** The director has agreed. The next thing will be discussion of the means by which you can have a solid career with a certain personal independence. Because of the great assistance you have been to us already, and because of a desire to give you some personal security, we want to give you an initial bank account of your own, and subsequently an annual working contract. In addition, because of the case [here Bagley mentioned Nosenko's unveiling of an important Soviet espionage agent whom I am not at liberty to identify], we are going to add an additional amount of money to the initial sum.

These promises, bogus though they proved to be, were of course being made to Nosenko by an agency that considered him an enemy agent, while across town J. Edgar Hoover, who himself was not known as credulous, considered Nosenko a valid defector. Hoover had in fact personally gone on record as believing that Nosenko's nemesis, Golitsyn, was a Soviet "provocateur" while at the same time expressing his confidence in Nosenko.

This conflict of views was compounded by the fact that the FBI would have liked more time to obtain all the valid information that they quite reasonably felt Nosenko might have. The position of the CIA, on the contrary, was that their prisoner (which he was in reality, even if not "officially") had to be kept isolated in order to prevent certain dimly sensed but never seen "KGB controllers" from masterminding his activities. At the same time they proceeded with the idea that Nosenko should, for the time being, be treated well enough to remain cooperative and debriefable. Unfortunately, the CIA won the battle, and from then on the FBI did not play any substantial role in the case.

As discussions continued at CIA headquarters the emphasis turned more and more to "breaking" Nosenko. Their aim, using whatever means might be required, was to induce him to confess that he was operating as part of a KGB "deception" operation. In April 1964 the agency therefore decided the only way to handle such a dangerous and unwelcome guest (who was nevertheless precious) was to lodge him in "escape-proof quarters" under armed guard twenty-four hours a day. When informed of the new arrangements Nosenko was understandably worried. His fear, as he later explained, was that the new arrangements were designed to milk him as rapidly as possible of all his information, after which he would be discarded without any haven or reward. Not only would he then find himself adrift in a strange land, he also actively feared that, once the CIA was rid of him, the KGB would be free either to kidnap or kill him. Little did Yuri know that his misgivings were as nothing compared with the agency's real intentions.

The plan conceived jointly by the CI staff and the SB division was a "heads you lose, tails you also lose" affair. It was assumed that Nosenko would almost certainly be eventually "broken" and thus forced to confess to some vast Machiavellian plot against the United States in which he himself would of course be a major player. Once he had confessed all, the intention was then to forcibly return him to Soviet hands. On the other hand, in the unlikely event that he was not "broken," the planners envisaged either the same fate or some equally unpleasant consequences. In any case, death by some means or other was foreseen as the inevitable result. The irony is, of course, that only if he had *lied* by admitting that he was still working for the KGB would his agency handlers have considered him to be telling the truth. But even then he probably would have been "liquidated" (to use a favorite word of his custodians). Thus, whatever he said or did, the consequences were to be a vicious retribution. He could not win!

As his tension and insecurity built up Nosenko nevertheless remained tractable and cooperative for awhile. Regrettably, as his fears increased he took to drinking throughout his waking hours.

THERE MUST BE A PLOT

We now must consider one of those peripheral incidents of history that is so often ignored, but which in the end becomes as important as the mainstream of events.

A much earlier Soviet defector, who had long been used as a CIA translator, was hard at work comparing the two records of Bagley's and Kisevalter's 1962 conversations with Nosenko—the actual tapes on one hand and the "transcripts" made of them on the other. A cursory review resulted in his pinpointing some 150 errors in the supposed transcripts, and he suggested there might be more. (As previously pointed out, these supposed transcripts were not literal word-for-word records of what had been said, but "impressionistic" English-language versions of what Kisevalter remembered of the many boozy conversations emanating from safe house meetings with Nosenko.)

Unhappily, although the existence of a revised version of the record that eliminated these numerous errors was made known to the operational team on 12 March 1964, there is no indication that anyone in a position of responsibility took advantage of it to clear up the misunderstandings. Truth, it seems, had become incidental. The essential objective of Bagley's team was to prove the existence of what those involved called a KGB "disinformation plot." If one then asks "What plot?" there can be no answer, because no such thing existed. The vicious theories spawned by Angleton, Bagley, and others were the product of undisciplined minds trying to cope with a reality that was intellectually beyond their grasp. The only gift any of the men involved possessed was the ability to fill a conceptual void with recondite-sounding words skillfully combined in preposterous sentences. Unfortunately, however, there was for some time no young boy on hand to notice that these latter-day emperors had no clothes.

Despite the pressure exerted by his interrogators, Nosenko displayed remarkable resolution in refusing to acknowledge deeds he had not committed. Such a display of fortitude, however, was not how his interrogators saw the matter. To them the obvious conclusion to be drawn was that even more pressure had to be put on him. No recreation of any kind could be allowed, nor any consideration given to the possibility that Nosenko might be telling the truth. The man was hoodwinking us, the interrogators believed, so the obvious response was confinement under what were euphemistically described as "spartan" circumstances. After that step had been arranged, a "hostile interrogation" was to ensue.

As it happened, the Soviets themselves presented a convenient model as to how to conduct that sort of thing. In late 1963 a Yale University professor, Frederick Barghoorn, while pursuing his studies in the Soviet Union had been accused of espionage and arrested by the

KGB. The conditions under which he had been detained, until he was released in response to a personal plea from President Kennedy, were duplicated in the CIA detention facilities provided for Nosenko. The original plan for the cell in which Nosenko was to be confined had no heat because there had been none in Professor Barghoorn's accommodations. The CIA Office of Security, however, whose role was subordinate in this affair but which nevertheless insisted on the maintenance of certain ethical and humanitarian standards, refused to go along with the idea of an unheated cell. That provision was therefore revoked. Another aspect of Barghoorn's confinement was a lack of air and light from the outdoors; what was proposed for Nosenko's window was to similarly obscure it by boarding it up. The only light in his cell was to be provided by one 60-watt bulb hanging from the ceiling, kept on day and night.

When it came time to incarcerate Nosenko he was told that he had "failed" a polygraph test just given him. This statement was self-evidently specious because the conditions under which the test was administered precluded a valid result; polygraph results are meaningless if the person being tested is artificially disturbed by threats or other emotional incitements. Nonetheless, once the test had supposedly been completed he was informed that he was being "arrested" because of his "lies." Upon being taken to his new and "spartan" quarters he was then ordered to strip and don prison clothes. From then on, as had been true in the professor's case, Nosenko was forced to arise at six in the morning and go to bed at ten at night, all the time with the light still burning. He was not allowed to lie down at all during the day, though he was graciously permitted to sit on his bed or on the one chair in his cell.

The meals initially prescribed for him were minimal:

Breakfast: weak tea, no sugar, porridge.
Lunch: watery soup, macaroni or porridge, bread.
Supper: weak tea and porridge.

Fortunately for Nosenko, a CIA doctor intervened to explain that this was a starvation diet, and the food was then slightly improved.

The intent, made explicit by Bagley and his colleagues, was to put Nosenko at a "psychological disadvantage" in order to shake his confidence and make him fearful. A twenty-four-hour visual surveillance was maintained by guards sitting outside his barred prison door. No physical mistreatment was involved (again a condition exacted by the Office of Security), but the guards were not to say a word to him and were instructed to treat him completely impersonally. In his presence they were never to smile.

Originally the only toilet facility was to have been a slop pail, which Nosenko himself would be forced to empty once a day. Again the Office of Security objected to this as well as to some other extreme provisions that were then rescinded. Particular emphasis was placed on the absolute prohibition against any "distractions." In addition to not being allowed to read, Nosenko was not allowed to hear a sound. The guards watching him round the clock were not to speak to him, nor even talk among themselves. They could watch television, as long as its screen was so oriented that Nosenko could not see it. And since their captive was not to hear the audio coming from it, they listened to the television through earphones. Although it had originally been planned to provide Nosenko with reading materials, this provision was reversed and he was allowed nothing. He became so starved for something to read, for any mental activity in fact, that upon finding a leaflet of instructions in a toothpaste wrapper he hid it under his blanket and tried to peruse it from time to time without being caught. No luck. It was quickly confiscated by his guards.

Had Yuri been a more ingenious person he might have asked for a Bible, either a Russian or English translation. To decorate one of his bare walls he might also have requested a crucifix. Such entreaties would have posed a dilemma for his jailers, and the Office of Security would almost certainly have intervened to see that his requests were granted. Yet, perhaps because he had been raised in a stratum of Soviet society in which overt religious manifestations were a violation of the political creed, he never posed any such problem for his persecutors. Locked in this void he nevertheless tried to keep track of the days by making a calendar out of threads torn from his clothing. But this effort, too, was foiled by the ever-vigilant security force which, by removing the threads out of which he had made the numbers, left him lost in a webless, timeless vacuum.

For a prolonged period—a total of about three years and two months—Nosenko was thus subjected to what is known to psychologists as sensory and perceptual deprivation (SPD), a state in which there is no visual, auditory, or mental stimulation. Research on this subject had begun in the United States and Canada in an effort to understand the psychological processes underlying the "brainwashing" used by the Chinese and North Koreans on Allied prisoners during the Korean War. One eminent authority has this to say about research on persons subjected to a stimulus-free environment:

> The results of this research were startling. The subjects, who were paid to do nothing except lie in a semi-soundproofed cubicle for several days and wear translucent goggles and listen to a constant masking sound of low intensity, reported a variety of unusual subjective phenomena such as vivid and highly structured hallucinations, delusions, and gross changes in the appearance of the perceptual environment upon emerging from isolation. In addition to these introspective reports, objective test data were obtained that [also] indicated an increased susceptibility to propaganda material, impairments in cognition and perceptual functioning, and a progressive slowing of occipital alpha frequencies with increasing duration of isolation.[3]

Note that the above-mentioned scientific experiments lasted only a few days. Nosenko, on the other hand, was subjected to more severe sensory deprivation over a period of *years,* in a situation aggravated by recurrent threats to his life. It is therefore remarkable that, although he did suffer from occasional delusional periods, neither his reason nor his consciousness was impaired for any prolonged period. This fact in itself implies that he possessed a much stronger character than his youthful indiscretions had seemed to indicate. He was to need every bit of that strength to survive what was still to come.

PUTTING THE SCREWS ON

In retrospect it is hard to understand the processes, both mental and bureaucratic, that could lead to the atrocity Nosenko endured. Let us look, therefore, at the organizational problems and pitfalls that brought it about, and consider the roles of some of the persons involved.

Richard Helms, supervisor of the agency's clandestine operations when Nosenko was first confined, became director of Central Intelligence in July 1966. In both capacities Helms had a great many concerns other than the Nosenko case, among them the war in Vietnam. If Helms could be faulted in any respect it would be for trusting the judgment of Jim Angleton, whose measure he should certainly have taken long before the mid-1960s. In fact Angleton was increasingly a gray eminence lurking mysteriously in the shadows of his dimly lit office, rather than an active operator. The secret of Angleton's survival under Helms must either have been that he bored Helms (and numerous directors before him) almost to death with his long-winded expositions, or, alternatively, that occasionally finding himself under challenge he always fell back on what I call the Prflovsky Ploy. This technique usually began with a blank, uncomprehending stare, followed by something to the effect that, "Of course, the Prflovsky case disproves that completely!" Since no one except Angleton, and perhaps one or two thoroughly cowed members of his staff, was likely ever to have heard of Prflovsky, the tactic usually ended any discussion at hand.

To complicate the bureaucracy even further, rather than Angleton's CI staff being in charge of the day-to-day managing of the Nosenko problem, the task had been assumed by the SB division, an arrangement due in part to the fact that although Angleton's staff specialized almost exclusively in Soviet matters, it had at the time to the best of my memory not a single Russian linguist in its ranks. Obviously—though it was not always done—Nosenko *should* have been handled by Russian speakers since he was not fluent in English.

Helms, however, had no particular reason to distrust any of the SB officers who took over the case, nor was he ever exposed to the relatively low-ranking people in the agency who took strong issue with the way the case was being handled. Had he been apprised of the extremism demonstrated by those in charge he would certainly have taken remedial measures. Regrettably no one brought these atrocities to his attention. For example, though Helms of course knew that Nosenko's confinement had been a long one, it was very late in the game before he discovered that during most of his time in detention, the Russian prisoner was not being interrogated, or even talked to, by either Bagley or other members of the CIA's operational team. In fact, records show that although Nosenko was incarcerated for a total of 1,277 days (approximately 42 months), only 292 days (9.7 months) were devoted in whole or in part to questioning him.

When Helms was at last informed that Nosenko had spent a quite substantial percentage of his imprisonment without being questioned or otherwise occupied, the memorandum addressed to him explained that "the interval in isolation will be extremely valuable in terms of allowing subject to ponder on the complete failure of his recent gambits." (What these "gambits" were is not clear; presumably the word refers to Nosenko's unwillingness to confess to crimes he had not committed.)

Even when Bagley was not talking to his prisoner, however, Nosenko was not far from his mind. As it happened this pensive case officer was given to sorting out his thoughts on paper, so for better or worse we know their tenor. One of these musings was devoted to the objectives of the interrogations that had taken place and that would no doubt be resumed in the future: "To gain more insight into points of detail which we could use in fabricating an ostensible confession. Insofar as we could make one consistent and believable even to the Soviets, a confession would be useful in any eventual disposal of Nosenko." Bagley subsequently generated a number of further thoughts on the same general subject, including: "To liquidate and insofar as possible to clean up traces of a situation in which CIA could be accused of illegally holding Nosenko." After that, "alternative actions" were listed, including: "Number five, liquidate the man. Number six, render him incapable of giving coherent story (special dose of drug, et cetera). Possible aim, commitment to loony bin. Number seven, commitment to loony bin without making him nuts." The fact that Bagley's time was dedicated to such ruminations indicates clearly that the attempt to "break" Nosenko had finally come to a dead end, thus suggesting a new question: Who would break first, the jailer or the jailed?

THE DIRECTOR LOSES PATIENCE

At last Dick Helms ran out of patience. Nosenko's confinement had begun on 6 April 1964, and on 23 August 1966 the director issued an ultimatum giving the investigators sixty days to wind up the job. (In fact, however, the process took considerably longer.) The result was a period of frenetic, though fruitless, activity on the part of Bagley's team. If, after two and a half years they had not been able to break the prisoner, how could they expect to do so in the remaining two months given to them?

Their first proposal was that Nosenko be reinterrogated, this time under the influence of sodium amytal, one of the drugs colloquially referred to as "truth serums." To their distress, however, Helms flatly refused to allow the use of any drug. The investigators were reduced to using, once again, the polygraph. Though the device had failed them before, it was the only weapon that remained in their arsenal to uncover the proof of Nosenko's evil intent that had so long eluded them. In fact, no mechanical contrivance can detect lies; all the polygraph machine does is register physiological changes as the person being tested responds to an examiner's questions. If skillfully and ethically employed it can be very useful. When wrongly used—as it was by Bagley's team, who were not under the jurisdiction of the CIA's highly professional Office of Security—it is at best useless and sometimes actually harmful.

The four processes measured by the polygraph are changes in blood pressure, pulse rate, respiratory rate, and skin conductivity to electricity. All four are responses to emotional stimuli, and if the person being tested is otherwise calm yet feels guilty about lying, his emotional reaction will vary from a baseline. (If the subject is not predisposed to feeling guilt, as is true of some habitual criminals, use of the polygraph is a waste of time.) The baseline is established at the beginning of the test by asking such unexciting questions as "What time is it?" or "What is your name?" Such questions give the examiner a measurement of the normal level or pace of the subject's physiological functions; from then on answers to crucial questions are measured in terms of variation from the norms thus obtained. Under no circumstances, however, should the examiner do anything in advance of the test that might induce tension; artificially generated tension will create unpredictable reactions and render the test meaningless.

Yet artificially inducing tension was exactly what the CIA team under Bagley's direct supervision intentionally did, both in connection with the 1964 polygraph examinations at the time Nosenko was first incarcerated and then in 1966 as a result of Helms's ultimatum. The team never did, in fact, even try to give their victim a valid test. Instead, their objective from the beginning was to reduce Nosenko's unusual level of physical and psychological stamina (which had enabled him to resist their accusations) through systematic and ongoing intimidation.

During one week, as Helms's sixty-day limit neared its end, the examining team submitted Nosenko to some twenty-eight-and-a-half hours of polygraphing, a repetitive process that by any professional standard is grossly excessive, particularly in that it artificially raises the subject's stress level. In addition, during the time he was not actually being questioned Nosenko was left strapped in a chair, his tension raised by uncertainty as to what would happen next, while the testing team took "breaks" for periods of as long as four hours.

On one occasion, in addition to being attached to the four regular sensors, a fifth contraption was attached to Nosenko's head. He was told this was an encephalograph, a device that could read his brain waves. The sole reason for introducing this artifact (which, in fact, was not part of an encephalograph at all) was that by raising Nosenko's tension they could engender tracings that could be interpreted as evidence of guilt. In other words, to *fabricate evidence*. During this time Nosenko was also verbally abused. In addition to calling him a "fanatic," one of the examining team members informed him that "your future is now zero." Remarkably, none of these variations from correct polygraph procedures were reported to higher supervisory levels of the agency. On the contrary, the written report made to the chief of the SB division spoke only of "significant reactions" on Nosenko's part, which in nontechnical language clearly implied "indications of guilt."

ABSOLUTION AT LAST

It is a pleasure to recount that Nosenko's ordeal did not end tragically. Thanks in part to his own strength of character, Nosenko eventually found the happiness and freedom that he had been seeking when he first arrived in our country. More important, for the welfare of both the United States and the agency itself, the tragic absurdity of the case fabricated against Nosenko was eventually brought to light and a return to sanity eventually came about.

Helms finally took the necessary measures to resolve the Nosenko problem in mid-1967. His first step was to hand responsibility over to his deputy, Vice Adm. Rufus Taylor, a superbly qualified intelligence officer and a thoroughly decent, civilized man. Rufe, as his friends knew him, brought in a professional from the agency's Office of Security, who promptly moved Nosenko out of his little prison cell. Though still confined for some time following, he was at least lodged in a comfortable and humane environment with people who had no compunction about smiling. Many months of reinterrogation followed, but the sessions were conducted under friendly circumstances by a man of normal human instincts who also knew his business.

The resultant report, issued in October 1968, accepted the obvious: Yuri Nosenko had been telling the truth ever since he first made contact with an American in 1962. As Director of Central Intelligence Admiral Stansfield Turner said in 1978, almost ten years later, "It was eventually determined that [Mr. Nosenko] had defected of his own free will, had not sought to deceive us, and had indeed supplied very valuable information to the U.S. Government. The hypothesis which had led to the original decision that he was misleading us was found to have been based on inadequate evidence." Yuri Nosenko now lives under an assumed name. He is married to a delightful lady of American birth, and has been employed by the CIA. In what capacity? Obviously, on matters relating to Soviet intelligence activities.

One of my own lasting memories of the six months I spent

examining the records of the Nosenko case is of an event that I chose not to submit when it came time for me to testify before a Congressional hearing. Looking around at the dignified assemblage in a large Capitol hearing room, the incident seemed beneath the dignity of the assembled group. Nonetheless, the event still sticks in my mind, and probably always will. The scene is my temporary CIA office in 1978, where Carol, an attractive American woman of Russian descent, was helping me understand a taped record of an interrogation conducted by Bagley in Nosenko's cell. At one point I could hear Nosenko's deep voice rumbling in Russian, his speech intermittently interrupted as if, somewhere down at the bottom of a deep well, he was sobbing. "What's all this about?" I asked. "He's saying," Carol replied, "'From my soul . . . from my soul . . . I beg you to believe me . . .'" And then there came the voice of Bagley, high-pitched in contrast to Nosenko's bass, screaming repetitively in English, "That's bullshit! That's bullshit! That's bullshit!"

Perhaps that little story will have some admonitory value for the men and women who, in the future, may contemplate an intelligence career. Its lesson is that there will be times when what they do is less important than what they do *not* do. Had Nosenko spun fantastic lies, he might have been believed; ironically, his undoing lay in telling the truth. Let me add the words I used in concluding my Congressional testimony regarding Nosenko: "I have had thirty-one years of government service, both military and civilian, [yet] it has never fallen to my lot to be involved with any experience as unpleasant as the investigation of this case. It was an abomination."

4
Mikhail
The Fabulist

AN APPROACH IN PARIS

For those who like novelty, a redeeming feature of the intelligence business is its occasional unpredictability. For the many others who prefer life to move at a regular rhythm and with few surprises, anything having to do with espionage is the wrong job. The latter was exactly the sentiment of the dignified gentleman who served as U.S. Army attaché in Paris in early January 1958 when he received an anonymous note that read: "Meet me at the Bar Chez François. Come in civilian clothes, and carry in your hand a copy of the newspaper *Sports et Vie*." The attaché did not finish reading the note, which was clearly the work of a "crank." Particularly distasteful to him was the presumption of the writer in telling him what to wear. He certainly would have given no more thought to the matter had he not a few days later been summoned to a meeting on this very subject in the office of the deputy chief of mission (DCM), second in command to the American ambassador. Also invited was "Bill," the senior CIA representative.

As the tale unfolded at this meeting, the writer of the letter did not give up easily and had made a second request for a meeting, this time by telephoning the attaché's office. Speaking in accented Spanish, the caller identified himself as a colonel in the army of an unspecified Latin American country and claimed to have in his possession military photographs that would be of interest to the United States. The DCM, a first-class man who later rose to be undersecretary of state, fully understood the importance of defectors and was not the sort to tolerate negativism. He let the attaché off the hook and ordered the CIA representative to assume responsibility for promptly contacting the caller.

Bill was fluent in Spanish and therefore decided to meet the man himself. He did, however, turn down Chez François as a meeting place, and the first conversation subsequently took place in a park not far from the embassy. Once face to face with an American official, the caller was revealed to be not a Latin American officer at all, but rather a Soviet colonel who spoke reasonably good, though highly accented, Spanish. His real name, irrelevant here, shall simply be changed to Mikhail.

Mikhail was surely the most unusual person that the CIA in Paris had been called upon to handle for some time. Though he carried a Mexican passport with a Spanish name, he immediately admitted his identification was counterfeit. Like the passport itself, the various visas it carried, ostensibly issued for entry into France and Italy by the French and Italian embassies in Mexico City, had in fact been forged by the GRU in Moscow. Finally, though Mikhail's passport said he was a Mexican citizen, he in fact had never been in Mexico—even for a visit.

What, then, was he up to? With no attempt at evasion he explained that he was a Soviet "illegal" (in this case a member of the Soviet military intelligence service, the GRU, assigned to France not in any official capacity), but disguised under a false, and unofficial, identity. Mikhail was ostensibly a businessman, though he claimed that his real assignment was to collect intelligence on "U.S. military personnel and activities in France, Italy, and Spain." On the face of it his posting to Paris was not unreasonable, since in 1958 the U.S. Armed Forces' European Command was located not far outside the French capital, and its activities were bound to be of great interest to the Soviet Union.

So far, so good. Yet Bill, a senior and experienced intelligence officer, questioned whether the Soviets would have documented someone as a Mexican if that person spoke Spanish incorrectly and with a strong Russian accent. The CIA had, with reason, great respect for the professionalism of the GRU, and this man's claims seemed in every way implausible. Intelligence services do strange things, particularly when dealing with areas about which they have only limited understanding. The operations officers in Paris vacillated, unable to come to a firm conclusion, for in the espionage business one encounters enough cranks and crooks to make one skeptical of mankind in general; in Mikhail's case suspicion seemed the order of the day. The CIA accordingly took everything he said with a grain of salt. He admitted that his passport was false—why not his whole story?

As a result, arrangements were made for this anomalous figure to be kept under surveillance day and night, a precaution that quickly revealed further discrepancies in his already incongruous story. For example, Mikhail had told Bill that he was required to maintain regular radio contacts with Moscow (for which he provided the frequencies and times), yet on one occasion when he should have been receiving a message from the GRU, U.S. surveillants watched him idly strolling down the streets with a pretty girl.

The CIA in Paris had better things to do and at that point would have liked to declare Mikhail a total fraud. Somewhat to their surprise, however, by this time one undeniable fact was available: GRU headquarters was transmitting encoded messages to him at regular intervals, and doing so on the fixed schedule he had disclosed.

Moreover, he had the equipment necessary to send messages to Moscow. There could thus be no doubt that, whatever his personal vagaries, the GRU did indeed consider him an agent. Whether or not he was properly carrying out his assigned duties in Paris was an entirely separate matter.

MIKHAIL'S BACKGROUND

Mikhail's answers to questions about his past—where did he come from? what was his family like?—seemed to shift kaleidoscopically along with his moods. Nevertheless, after reiterative debriefings a more or less coherent picture eventually emerged. He claimed to have been born in Moscow in 1922. "That year my father was in the last contingent of troops fighting for the Old Russia. He was then [transferred to] the Far East, and naturally I could not have known him. As I later learned, he went to the U.S.A. I have had no news of him since." Just before the outbreak of World War II, he said, he had graduated from a school for military-political officers (often called "political commissars"), just as Oleg Penkovsky had, but he claimed no other military training. He never saw combat during the entire war, but with obvious pride he remarked that, "I have no military or Party reprimands, and never was the subject of court martial or investigation." This boast became a joke among the officers involved in the case, and one can imagine their exclaiming, "And he doesn't beat his wife, either!"

With greater justification he proudly spoke of having received further military-political education after the war, and of eventually becoming head of a military "university," where he reached the rank of lieutenant colonel. In 1953, however, he discovered that he was to be demoted (not in rank, but in the importance of his position) to being a mere army division political officer. When he protested he was assigned to the GRU instead. That service then submitted him to some four years of military intelligence training (much like Popov's), after which he was assigned for eight months to East Berlin.

Once in Berlin, Mikhail's assignment, as he described it, was as implausible as was so much else about him. In that old German-speaking Prussian capital he was ordered to perfect his Spanish—an improbable story, on the face of it. And yet, as Bill could testify, Mikhail *did* speak that language fluently, even while making frequent errors. "Yes," Mikhail explained, "I was told to improve my Spanish by getting acquainted with a person of Spanish extraction, so that I could meet with this person in my free time." Had he himself located that "person"? No, the center had selected a certain woman, and he went on to describe her in glowing terms: "She is a very beautiful Spanish girl! There is no point in concealing that I formed a close relationship with her. . . . I was able to speak Spanish with her all the time!" If one could believe his story, his efforts to learn a new language had been so highly valued that he was thereafter promoted to full colonel on the basis of "my impeccable military record and background."

CAREER AS AN ILLEGAL

In June 1956 Mikhail began his career as an illegal in Western Europe. Though his comings and goings may at first seem bizarre, what he claimed to have accomplished did in fact follow the pattern of Soviet agents establishing themselves under commercial cover in a foreign land, and his story was thus believable. Upon leaving Berlin he had traveled to Switzerland where, as the bearer of a Mexican passport, he had no trouble registering as a businessman. Apparently the GRU had already made ample funds available to him, which in talking to the Swiss authorities he ascribed to an inheritance from his father. Once established in Switzerland he then further covered his tracks by moving on to France (again, this was not unusual for an illegal). There at long last he could establish himself as the representative of a Swiss business firm in the area of his intelligence target: the mammoth U.S.

military headquarters located on the outskirts of Paris.

To the CIA men debriefing him that chapter of Mikhail's life passed muster, because it conformed to standard GRU procedure in setting up illegals. Their cover was normally built step by step, establishing an intercontinental trail of false identities, counterfeit documentation, and bogus organizations that busy immigration and police officials generally did not have the time or inclination to unravel unless strong evidence of a crime existed. Crime was not among Mikhail's many weaknesses, but carelessness was.

Mikhail's reason for trying to contact the American military attaché centered around a need for money, and that in turn was due partly to an automobile accident. Unfortunately Mikhail's errors tended to be on a grand scale, and his accident accordingly took place at the Place d'Etoile, Paris's majestic central circle where several avenues converge at the Arc de Triomphe. Not only did he completely wreck his own car (rented in Switzerland) but he also badly damaged the taxi he hit. The French police, always in full force at the Etoile, judged that the collision was entirely his fault. As a result he owed thousands of dollars, both to the Swiss car rental firm and to a French taxi company. Unfortunately, however, due to liberal expenditures for his own pleasures, the fund allowed for his intelligence operations was severely depleted and explained why he had decided to contact the U.S. military attaché.

Aside from Mikhail's extravagant living and carelessness at the wheel, once having set up his cover (the easiest part of his assignment), how successful had his intelligence-collection mission been as of the time he volunteered to cooperate with the United States? That was at first difficult to determine because a blanket of mystery had been thrown over much of what he was up to. Mikhail carefully controlled the dates, times, and length of meetings whenever a case officer contacted him, and evasively claimed that he had no time to answer detailed questions. Rigid security precautions were essential, he said, in case the GRU was surveilling him. A dispatch written at the time was not encouraging: "Getting accurate information from Mikhail is difficult, and to date we do not even have documentary proof of the name he was given at birth."

One simple question must have dogged the Americans' thoughts: What was the GRU itself really up to? What possible role could a Spanish-speaking Russian pretending to be a businessman (while knowing little about business) play in penetrating the secrets of one of the most heavily guarded military headquarters in Europe? At first glance the answer seemed clear: none. Yet how could one even be sure that Mikhail had actually been put in place for the purpose the GRU had specified in their instructions to him? Was Paris just another way station on the long trail to his real destination? Was he simply being tested in order to ensure that he could be trusted with another, more realistic mission? Who could say the GRU might not, on short notice, revise his mission and send him to an area where Spanish was the principal language spoken?

Perhaps the GRU center itself had misgivings, because less than three months after he first contacted the U.S. Army attaché it broadcasted instructions for Mikhail to come back to Moscow for "consultation." Typically, however, he had not returned to his Paris apartment by the hour designated for the receipt of this urgent message, and was therefore unaware of it until the Paris CIA office, having already decoded it, passed it to him. To be so suddenly summoned back to the center implied that Mikhail was in trouble, and the Americans involved were actually relieved at the thought that the GRU might scrub his so-called "operation" and keep him safely at home. But no such luck. To their surprise he was back in Paris by mid-April 1958. Submitted promptly to a stern CIA interrogation, Mikhail remained as unrepentant as he was evasive. The CIA's only consolation was that its officers seemed at last to be making some progress in categorizing Mikhail's lies.

A considerable number of those lies appeared to stem simply from Mikhail's desire to maintain a certain level of dignity. For example, perhaps he thought that his many liaisons with young women were not compatible with his status as a family man—"head of family," as he sometimes pompously and hierarchically described himself. When first questioned he had explained that, having been in the army since he was eighteen, he and his wife had never really had much life together, nor did they have children. In fact it eventually emerged that not only had he *not* moved as frequently as he had alluded, but he also had a young son. Moreover, his wife frequently sent him affectionate messages via the GRU radio link.

Other deceptions stemmed from his desire to inflate his own importance. It was never known for certain, for example, whether his claim to having been promoted to the rank of full colonel was true. He was so totally unconcerned with truth and so immersed in an illusionary universe that it appeared that once he had convinced himself of his own confabulations, he no longer lived in the real universe but rather in a world of lies, not the least of which may have been those he told himself. Although Mikhail was supposed to be a businessman, most of his associates were women. Not businesswomen somehow related to his cover story, but women whom he sought out purely for pleasure. Above all they usually were simple women, not sufficiently educated to fathom his fakery.

There was Teresa, the nineteen-year-old daughter of a Brazilian consular official and a Russian gypsy mother. "A beautiful girl with long black hair," Mikhail enthused. She danced in a gypsy nightclub and Mikhail's phone calls to her were punctuated by clumsy flattery and embarrassed giggles. There was Zara, an Iranian, before whom Mikhail flaunted his U.S. dollars while spinning myths about his nonexistent sister in Spain who was purportedly married to an equally fictitious prince. His most stable liaison, however, was with a French woman, Danielle, who lived with him and bore him a child. Their relationship was nevertheless not a close or consistent one, and she was left to wonder why, at certain more-or-less fixed times, her companion put on a headset and listened to a radio. There were also other interruptions of their domestic bliss. On at least one occasion when a male visitor arrived, Mikhail unceremoniously ordered Danielle out of the apartment, and she could do nothing but stroll the streets while waiting to be readmitted to what she thought was their home. It appears the visitor was an intelligence contact of some sort, though Mikhail could hardly explain this to his consort and made no attempt to do so. Poor Danielle. Like all his women, she shared Mikhail's ejaculations but little else.

Despite the fact that he was liberally funded by Moscow, did Mikhail actually perform any useful function on behalf of the GRU? Not as far as his American case officers could discern. Like Pyotr Popov he seemed unable to apply any of what he had been taught during his GRU training, yet unlike Popov he was not amenable to American guidance. His own attempts to develop intelligence-gathering operations were pitiful, and of no use to either Russia or the United States—and so they remained until the end.

It almost goes without saying that the showpiece among what purported to be his "operations" centered around a woman. "I want to show Moscow that I have agents who can provide me with information," he pontificated on one occasion. "So, after solidifying my position in Paris, I began to search for persons whom I could report to Moscow. . . . I found such a person who has a job in the headquarters of one of the armies in which I am interested." He was referring to the American army, of course, though he liked to magnify his target by talking about "armies." "This person," he continued proudly, "is Zoë. She is Russian by origin. How did I become acquainted with her? In Paris there is a small Russian restaurant and one day I met her there. In talking to her, I learned she works in a military unit, by a telephone, and can overhear conversations!"

So far so good, except that Zoë turned out to be nothing more than a clerk employed at a U.S. Army motor pool located near Fontainebleau, out in the Paris suburbs where the U.S. headquarters was located. The only reason Mikhail confided this speciously "top secret" tidbit was that his invaluable female agent had tired of suburban living and was planning to move into central Paris. Mikhail wanted his American case officer to forestall her move, presumably by intervening with the U.S. Army organization employing her.

The account of Zoë's importance was comic, yet Mikhail's anxiety became evident as he explained, "I have already reported about her to Moscow and been ordered to keep her in place. She is much valued by Moscow, because it is very difficult to recruit such a person!" Despite his four years of training this senior GRU officer was utterly unable to evaluate realistically the value of a supposed "agent" who, however pleasant she may have been in bed, could not have been of the slightest use in an intelligence capacity. Interestingly, however, Mikhail did not make as much of an impression on Zoë as she did on him. The CIA eventually learned from an independent source that though she had accepted several invitations to have dinner and had probably slept with him, Mikhail had never made clear that he wanted her to collect intelligence. Indeed, from her standpoint the relationship had been a rather casual one. Though she recalled that he had offered to find her a better job, when later questioned about him she could not remember his address, telephone number, or even last name.

An Unproductive Operation for All

One might ask why the agency wasted so much time on Mikhail. That question can only be answered by countering with another: Why did Mikhail's tough-minded superiors in the GRU waste *their* time on him? Beyond any doubt they had spent a good deal of effort on his training, were devoting time to communicating with him by radio, and were providing money for his "operations." Equally beyond any doubt, this hopeless dilettante simply squandered the considerable sums provided by Moscow.

Speaking from my own experience, intelligence operations conducted long distance via brief coded messages are unrealistic unless highly motivated people are involved at both ends. It takes unusual devotion for a singleton agent to take the risks involved in recruiting agents in a hostile territory unless he knows that his performance will be periodically checked by some higher authority. Unfortunately for the GRU, their rules forbade direct on-the-spot contact with an illegal, an arrangement from which Mikhail temporarily benefited and his superiors lost. It apparently took them some time to realize the extent of his malfeasance. Despite his sophisticated external appearance, Mikhail was emotionally quite immature. He considered himself and his desires most important, and had a subjective yardstick in dealing with other people. He would play along with them only as long as their aims paralleled his own, and he would change immediately when a better deal was offered. He had little capacity for establishing emotional contacts with others. He had almost no self-doubts or compunctions, and went about his business in a rather brazen way. When it suited his purposes he would claim to be a decent and honest person, whereas in reality he had neither a feeling for ethical principles or for loyalty. If the GRU had had a capability for psychological analysis of its agents, they would not have sent this hapless blunderer abroad.

Like Popov, Mikhail appears to have had no premonition of his unhappy end. From Penkovsky, however, the CIA learned that he was eventually called home, tried, and executed.

5
Motivation
What Manner of Men Are These?

THE NEW SOVIET MAN

"Inconstancy, hesitation, and laziness, those are my enemies," Leo Tolstoy once said of himself. He died in 1910, having spoken regretfully not only of his own generation but of others long gone, and he seemed hardly more optimistic about those still to come. What Tolstoy would have thought of the "new men" who arose with the Revolution is hard to say.

The Soviets I studied in some depth in order to write this book were purportedly all of a new breed, trying hard to fit the officially prescribed Soviet mold, at least on the surface. As such they were supposed to be the opposite of Russia's pre-Revolutionary middle- and upper-class dilettantes. To the Communists who had come to power with Lenin, the average Russian was an inefficient instrument for the building of a new and better world—overly emotional and susceptible to strongly accentuated mood swings, men who gave way easily and all too openly to depression and despair. The typical Russian might intellectually accept the need to control his impulses but he was nevertheless prone to excessive indulgence. At times he would work hard, but only in fits and starts, and often take refuge in strong drink.

To remedy these defects the Soviets decided to draw on a northern and central European model. The hoped-for new man was to resemble nothing so much as a dour fin de siècle Scot or German: formally dressed, stiff in manner, ponderous in speech, and prudishly proper in regard to sex. In action he would be hardworking, self-disciplined, emotionally undemonstrative, strict with subordinates, and unquestioningly loyal to direct superiors, to the Party, and to the state, but also abundantly endowed with energy and determination to succeed. Above all else he would not question orders.

Such a goal, it must be admitted, was asking a bit much, and quite understandably the Soviets never completely achieved their original aim of negating "antisocial" impulses. Until their regime's collapse, however, Soviet leaders managed to enforce criteria of behavior that outwardly were respected by all (except the punctilious actions of a few mavericks like Khrushchev). In doing so they greatly accelerated the process of Europeanization of their country begun by Peter the Great, and thus made it possible for a man of peasant origins like Popov eventually to feel comfortable in non-Communist central Europe—up to a point.

Imposing the model on all citizens was from the beginning one of the principal tasks of the Party, and it is interesting to note that many of the CIA's Soviet spies had themselves, at one time or another, been part-time enforcers. From what we know of their personalities they could quite easily and successfully do so because they enjoyed performing any role that carried with it an aura of power and prestige. Yet they sometimes played their social role without much real comprehension of its attendant responsibilities. This lack of recognition is reflected in the following story, told by a man I call Nikolai, who attributed it to the famous Soviet aircraft designer, Oleg Konstantinovich Antonov:

I [Antonov] arrived in Moscow and went for a walk. On the way I saw that a building was being put up, so went close to see what was being done. A truck comes up full of bricks, and two girls begin unloading by throwing the bricks on a pile. Obviously, so handled the bricks break up. . . . The girls who did the unloading said that they were not responsible for the bricks; all they were answerable for was how many truckloads they unloaded.

Then, I asked the truck driver what was going on. The latter answered that he gets paid on the basis of how many truckloads he delivers. . . . All these other things are no affair of his!

"The bricks?" Nikolai mused Socratically. "No one was interested in them. This example, of course, applies to the entire Soviet Union."

To judge from the Soviet Union's progress in some fields, particularly space exploration and defense, Antonov's anecdote does not seem to have represented the state of affairs of the entire nation, at least in his day. As conditions in the USSR continued to deteriorate, on the other hand, it does seem increasingly prophetic. Whatever the situation may in fact have been, however, the CIA's secret agents were rarely willing to give their compatriots much credit for good performance. In that respect and in nearly every other way, their feelings toward their country as a whole were always antagonistic.

Another consideration is that although pressure from earliest childhood to conform to an ideal model of duty and discipline may not have achieved the desired results in terms of civic rectitude, it certainly seems to have resulted in a widespread neurosis born of strongly conflicting impulses. I suggest that one consequence of this conflict has been the epidemic alcoholism in the Soviet Union, but that it is not the only one. There are numerous ways to resolve psychological conflict other than getting drunk and, for the Soviets mentioned in this book, one of those alternatives appears to have been treachery. Supporting this contention is the fact that, unlike many of their countrymen, almost all the Soviet spies I studied—with the principal exception of Yuri—were quite moderate in their consumption of alcohol; treachery may therefore have served as an alternative way of resolving their inner tensions and conflicts while at the same time bringing in enough extra money to finance a double—and more agreeable—life.

The preceding chronicles of the activities of individual Soviet officers have been largely descriptive. Yet the soldiers have paraded by without our learning much about why they march. No wonder. For reasons of survival, spies are secretive people; much as some birds have plumage that keeps them inconspicuous, spies have deceptive pretensions. Our understanding has, of course, not been helped by some of the media myth-merchants who profit by glorifying these individuals as strong, violence-prone, oversexed, often handsome, and certainly decisive.

Let us here try to undo the distortions, and look more closely at just what made certain Soviet spies function as they did.

PYOTR POPOV

Such further light as can be shed on Popov is based on CIA psychological tests, as well as inferences that can be made from his life story as he himself recounted it. The latter, however, was volunteered in a largely haphazard manner; his statements must be accepted as those of a simple, nonintrospective man. As time passed we probably understood him better than he understood himself.

In searching for clues to his disloyalty to the Soviet regime, we know as much from history as from what Pyotr told us. One thing that stands out is the lack of respected authority figures to whom Pyotr could look during his childhood, for like many of the Soviets who later defected he had lost his father early in life and his mother seems to have exercised little influence on him. As a dominant figure in the family there remained only his dynamic brother, Aleksandr. Aleksandr comes through Pyotr's story hard as rock and not particularly affectionate, though he was certainly interested in his younger sibling's welfare and for a while played a major role in shaping Pyotr's future.

Presumably the small boy's schoolmaster was also an authority figure, for he was a person much admired in the locality. Since the school was not even in Pyotr's village, however, the teacher would have cast a distant and perhaps even frighteningly authoritative shadow. Before the Revolution, of course, there also had been a dimly known, faraway personage, the Tsar, barely distinguishable from God Himself; if ordinary working people ever saw this kindly, bearded man they were likely to get down on their knees and pray. By the time Popov was old enough to be conscious of such matters, however, that temporal ruler had been wafted away on the winds of war and revolt; and as to the Deity, the commissars did not approve of Him. No doubt people who kept an icon in their house even after the Revolution, as the Popov family did, still nevertheless murmured their thanks to God because He at least lent some meaning and structure to their small universe. Yet what, realistically, did they have to thank Him for?

A study sponsored by Harvard University of the early post-Revolutionary period says that, as he reported his own experience, "the peasant is outstandingly the most oppressed, exploited, and disadvantaged man of the Soviet era."[1] Peasants did as they were told by the authorities, who could enforce their will by armed persuasion if necessary. Yet the peasants' obedience often stemmed more from their will to survive than out of respect for those who gave orders. This pattern is important, because the prevalent yet self-contradictory duality of obedience versus disrespect for the authorities helps explain the nonchalance with which Popov later accepted his life as a U.S. agent while simultaneously continuing to aspire to promotion within the Soviet officer corps. Putting his personality in a slightly different framework, one immediately realizes that Popov must have learned to dissemble, to pretend that he was something he was not, simply because all his life that behavior pattern had been the key to survival under the Soviet regime. Beneath the neat uniform he eventually wore he always felt himself a peasant, even if the Soviet social system gradually taught him to take on superficially the modes and manners of an officer—a behavior pattern based largely on tsarist precepts that, once adopted, continued without much change after the Revolution.

As to Popov's lack of commitment to the Communist system versus his outward conformity to its rules, it may be tempting to believe that his disloyalty to the Soviet state was greater than the norm because of the influence of his rebellious brother, Aleksandr. Yet it appears that Pyotr's attitude may in fact have been typical for one who came of peasant background. "The peasant is outstanding in his punitive attitude toward the leadership of the Soviet Union," the Harvard study says. "About 75 percent of this group advocate violent death for the top leaders [of the Soviet Union], and about 80 percent are willing to drop an atom bomb on Moscow."[2] In relation to the more basic aspects of his own society, on the other hand, Popov maintained a strong bond nevertheless. His personality had been formed by growing up among his fellow peasants on the hard land; it was all they knew. Though much in Popov's family's life had been as difficult as the soil they tilled, there were also pleasant things to remember—among them the neatness and order that was part of going to school. Above everything else Pyotr liked simplicity and peace.

The principal bond between Pyotr and his country was therefore not religion, because he had none, but merely a simple tradition of decency, cleanliness, and harmony, in addition to the language by which one thought about such uncomplicated matters. To him, obviously, "language" meant Russian. Though later in life he learned two other idioms, he never mastered either well enough to partake fully of a foreign culture. One of the attractions of Mili was that they could chat in Serbian, a language closely akin to Russian. Certainly the American case officer Kisevalter would not have been so much a friend to Pyotr had he not spoken Russian as easily as he did.

The cleanliness and decency of his home within a peasant community did nothing to prepare Popov for what was to come. We have already described the new Soviet man as envisaged by Communist doctrinaires, and for better or worse Pyotr knew he would never come close to conforming to this model except in the most superficial way. The best he could do in trying to rise to the demands imposed upon him was to be polite, calm, alert, and conventionally intelligent (at least on the surface). These qualities were all evident when agency officers first met him. On the other hand they also noted that he chewed his nails, suffered from high blood pressure, was systematically unfaithful to his wife, and chronically lied to his superiors. Then, when he feared that his derelictions might be discovered, he would break into tears. In other words, to the very last he was never at ease with the pseudo-personality he had developed to conceal his humble origins and weaknesses of character.

Both aspects of this dichotomous psyche were, by adulthood, inherent and real. The polite, composed, disciplined, and superficially forceful military officer was the product of long education and indoctrination. One cannot deny that Pyotr had learned some of his lessons well, for had not this simple peasant boy achieved senior military rank? Had he not also become Communist Party secretary in several of the units to which he was assigned? While he often talked to George, his American case officer, about the inequities of the Communist system (especially its treatment of the peasantry), his political attitudes were nevertheless in other respects quite orthodox; "above all," he said on one occasion, he craved "order, discipline, and dignity." Yet there was another patently visible side to his character. A CIA psychologist described Pyotr as a "delayed adolescent," by which he meant that by middle age he had still not resolved many of his conflicting impulses, a number of which were still childishly short-sighted and self-indulgent.

Such continued immaturity, it may be hypothesized, is frequently the result of a lack of a firm father figure in early life. His father was dead and his rebellious brother Aleksandr was gone, which left young Popov with only his mother, who survived her husband for just a few years. There is no reason to think she wielded much authority over him, however; during his youth in a man's world the normal pattern for Soviet mothers was one of simple indulgence. Thus he received no more discipline than he would have as an orphan. With Aleksandr's departure Pyotr had in effect lost two fathers in succession, and spiritually he was doubly orphaned. In that respect he was not unusual since the First World War, followed by the Revolution, had taken an enormous toll of both Russian men and women. Stalinist repression and World War II may have done away with as many as forty million more.

Many young men like Popov, having had their families dissolved by death or abandonment, quickly found that in this catastrophic era the Soviet system could not afford to indulge them. The authorities had no time for sympathy, nor could they dole out much by way of succor. The Darwinian principle that only the fittest survive was thus in full force, and people such as Pyotr found salvation could be achieved by one means alone: through successfully making one's way step by step upward via a ladder of organizations—schools, the Komsomol (Communist Union of Youth), and the Party itself, with its many gradations of acceptance. To be admitted to the Party was a rare honor, yet one that Pyotr achieved. It was the safest haven available. Nothing could better attest to his ability to dissemble, however, for he hadn't the slightest faith in its doctrines.

Though the impulse to achieve Communist Party status could for many people be a matter of idealism, at least as many believed that the formalistic honors stemming from Party membership were simply a matter of practical advantage. In a country struggling to remake itself completely life was lived at the narrow margin between survival and death. For most of the population there was every reason to conform. Like Pyotr, many did so without conviction, without much patriotism, and exclusively in their own interest.

Until, that is, the Germans invaded the motherland—an event that united Russians as none other had since the Napoleonic era. For a few years the world changed, even for people like Popov. Except during his war service, a period about which we know little, Popov fitted neatly into a moderately derogatory category that has quite a different meaning in Russian than in English: he was a "careerist." The Soviet nation was really too large to efficiently select its hierarchy, a fact that was implicitly admitted during frequent public complaints against people who by glibness and artifice satisfied governmental requirements in a token fashion. The word "careerist" was therefore invented to describe conformists who were also actively upwardly mobile but lacked any genuine loyalty to their society. Pyotr certainly belonged in this category.

Unfortunately for him, however, once abroad and required to apply his extensive training in practical situations, he wasn't very good at pushing his way upward. Lacking much understanding of the strange German-speaking world into which the Soviet Army had plunged him, he was in fact helpless to the point that his American case officers had to guide him through all but the most routine of assignments. Their assistance enabled him to survive on the margin of acceptability in his capacity as a Soviet intelligence officer, but not much more.[3]

He seems to have shone in the context of an eternal "good student" who learned his lessons carefully, even though he had little or no interest in their content—probably the characteristic that eventually won him the position of Communist Party secretary within his unit in Vienna. The position was a prestigious job in which he was supposed to function as guardian of his colleagues' ideological purity. He no doubt carried out his Party duties in an undemanding fashion, which probably suited his fellow officers, many of whom do not seem to have been any more politically dedicated than he. The pattern of ingratiation was so deeply imbedded in him that any Party meetings over which he helped preside must have been low-key, pro forma affairs.

Popov's lack of assertiveness and his eternal politeness carried over to his relations with his American case officers. He never fawned, but was deferential to a fault—even asking their permission before he combed his hair. His appearance, speech, and manners were nevertheless so deceptive that when he arrived in Vienna his superiors could justifiably take him for a model Soviet officer. On paper his record was excellent. He had been wounded in action during the war, graduated from two prestigious academies, and reached the rank of major; he was not only a Party member but a secretary; he was neat and military, wrote a fine hand, was a crack shot, and never got falling-down drunk. Since the GRU at that point had a personnel structure heavily weighted with slots for senior officers, his prospects for advancement were bright. Indeed, he was quickly promoted to lieutenant colonel. After that, what went wrong?

One clue is revealed by psychological tests routinely administered by the CIA, which showed him to be almost completely "self-absorbed." In simpler terms, even those few he loved were secondary to his own well-being. His problems arose from the fact that, once in Vienna, he was no longer subject to the same constraints he had felt within the Soviet Union. Moreover, his new duties as an intelligence officer, within which he was encouraged to be secretive, allowed him a degree of freedom enjoyed by few other Soviets, civilian or military. Taking full advantage of this new-found liberty, he gave free reign to his basic impulses.

Pyotr quickly and easily took to his liberation because he had little in common with his brother officers. Almost all of them came from city families and were of somewhat superior education and wider culture. Unfortunately Popov was deeply uncomfortable among those more sophisticated than himself, and he admitted to his case officers that he preferred people who actually looked up to him, as the population of his village did whenever he returned there. Such adulation his fellow officers had no reason to express. Quite the contrary, in fact.

With the advent of World War II the Soviet Army had reverted almost completely to the class-conscious rules and customs of tsarist times, as evoked by shoulder boards bearing rank insignia, innumerable orders and medals to string across one's chest, and increasingly elaborate uniforms. At the same time the army became if anything even more exigent than the Party in its demands that everyone conform to the model of the new man: "The routine of discipline within the officer corps is rigorous," says one author. "To fail to correct a junior for not saluting properly can bring punishment. Yet a salute rendered [by a subordinate] may be returned by a contemptuous glance, or not at all. Orders are given with deliberate harshness. In conference, only the senior speaks except by permission."[4]

In this stratified aristocracy there existed none of the cozy chumminess found in some officer corps in which the barriers of rank relax appreciably during off-duty hours. On the contrary, it became increasingly difficult for a peasant boy like Popov to find any comfortable niche among his compatriots. As a substitute for the unpalatable companionship of his fellow officers, Popov found Mili.

Milica Kohanek was an undemanding exile from the Serbian region of Yugoslavia. With her Popov could spend many of his off-duty hours—and probably some hours when, ostensibly, he was on duty. In terms of Popov's life, finding this friend was a turning point; though Mili never knew what she had accomplished (and might have been horrified if she had), she finally made it necessary for Pyotr to throw himself on the mercy of the CIA.

He had been living far beyond his means even before his affair with Mili began, and their unwedded bliss only increased his financial

difficulties. According to one of his case officers Popov was eventually reduced to using GRU operational funds for her support. All his difficulties were not ascribable to his mistress, however. The basic
problem was finding himself exposed for the first time in his life to the
temptations of a great cosmopolitan city like Vienna, and not knowing how to resist them.

Desperately Popov began looking for a remedy, and what could
have been more natural than for him to turn to the Americans who,
in the Austria of the early postwar years, symbolized wealth? Why
should he then not simply accost a U.S. officer on the street? Soviet
intelligence personnel in Vienna had all been cautioned to beware of
the Americans, who employed their evil dollars to subvert foreigners.
Yet to Popov that possibility presented no threat. On the contrary, it
was exactly the opportunity he was seeking.

Popov worked out well as a CIA agent because our treatment and
direction of him were the exact opposite of the kind he routinely
received from his Soviet superiors. The latter assumed that because he
had been trained at the Military-Diplomatic Academy, he already
knew his trade. They did not take account of the fact that, although
as a good rote learner he was able to parrot the words he had memo-
rized at the Academy, he had little concept of what those words meant
in practice. Thus, no matter how many orders his Soviet superiors
barked at him, he simply didn't know how to put them into effect.

The agency's approach, on the other hand, was more responsive
to his needs. Popov's American case officers correctly assumed igno-
rance, and therefore discussed every problem with him at great length
but in simple terms. Moreover, there was a warmth to the relationship
that he craved deeply. Kisevalter, the bilingual American, became the
nearest thing to an affectionate father he had ever known. Popov
would have tried to climb any mountain for George, and indeed he
eventually died trying to reach a peak beyond his capabilities.

OLEG PENKOVSKY

Oleg Vladimirovich Penkovsky shared with Popov the trauma of being an orphan, but the resemblance between the two stops there. Nonetheless, in one important respect they were alike: both were experts at dissembling—in other words, at projecting an image of themselves that was often far from the real person. This similarity between the two men is crucial to the fact that, though they emerged from totally different backgrounds, both became successful spies.

Because Penkovsky considered himself what we might call "upper middle class," he preferred to think of himself as an "aristocrat." Oleg can in fact be understood only by recognizing that during his lifetime the urban class structure of the Soviet Union, despite the regime's propaganda, was to a large extent an evolution and amplification of that which already existed in tsarist times; even prior to the Revolution it had been moving steadily in the same direction as that of Western Europe.[5] With increasing industrialization and universal education, "by the late thirties, the Soviet Union had a social class structure which was very much like that in the other major industrial countries of Europe and America. True, there were no landowning or industrialist upper classes, and no nobility, but there was an analogous class [consisting largely of the Party hierarchy and bureaucracy], which lived on a relatively lavish scale. . . . The class system thus established . . . has become greatly strengthened during the decade 1940 to 1950."[6] Those ideas, written in 1959, are still generally valid.

Concretely, we have only Penkovsky's tale about his upper-class origins, plus two pictures of his well-dressed and sophisticated-looking parents, to support what he said. Nonetheless, we know that the KGB's first suspicions in regard to him were triggered by the discovery of what were described as "aristocratic origins" and his father's service in a White Russian, that is, pro-tsarist army during and after the Revolution.[7]

Psychologically, it is important to note that Penkovsky always alluded to the disappearance of his father in a context clearly implying the loss of his birthright as a hereditary member of a ruling class. His deprivation was later aggravated when the KGB discovered his origins; the discovery led him to be removed from active duty in the army and assigned as a civilian to the GNTK. Thus, while Popov may be thought of as having lost two father figures in succession, Oleg Penkovsky suffered a double loss of status. One could safely suggest that to a considerable degree his behavior thereafter stemmed from his anger born of this deprivation.

Why certain people more actively seek, and even require, superiority of rank and social status than do others is not a question psychologists have addressed with much success. In Penkovsky's case, however, he probably had been imbued from childhood by his mother with the idea that the Communists had deprived him of his birthright.[8] His status insecurity was evidenced, for example, when he asked his case officers what his American diplomatic counterparts in Turkey had thought of him, then later wanted to know what impression he had made on "Sir Richard." Penkovsky's endless quest for reassurance appears to have been a reaction to a deeply felt uncertainty as to his intrinsic value as a human being. In addition to his social insecurity, the fact that he had to treat the truth about his upper-class heritage as a damning piece of evidence probably forced him from childhood into a neurotic mold. Every day of keeping the secret of what he called his "hereditary nobility" merely added fuel to the fire of his quest for honor and superiority in other domains. World War II may thus in fact have been a boon to Penkovsky, as it was to many Soviets, because for a while one's antecedents were forgotten; during those war years he and all his compatriots were temporarily accepted on the basis not of who they were but of what they could do to defend their country. Even certain high-ranking victims of Stalin's purges of the military leadership were rehabilitated, such as

Penkovsky's uncle, who rose to a rank equivalent to a U.S. lieutenant general. Many previously expropriated *kulaks,* some of whom had been resettled in the cities, also found acceptance. During this wartime period Penkovsky, having become an outwardly ardent member of the Communist Party, never missed an opportunity to ingratiate himself with the higher echelons of the military—toadying to Varentsov, for example, and marrying the daughter of another high-ranking officer, Lieutenant General Gapanovich. Capable, industrious, and sycophantic when he needed to be, by the end of the war Penkovsky's continued rise seemed assured.

Unfortunately, however, he could not tolerate even a temporary frustration of his boundless ambitions. His eventual reduction in status upon the arrival of the permanent *rezident* in Ankara had been foreseen from the outset, and was an entirely routine process. To him it nevertheless came as a crucial blow. At first the secretive side of his double nature took over, as he made anonymous phone calls to the Turkish counterintelligence service. Then his anger swelled to such proportions that he could no longer keep his feelings to himself. His message through KGB channels, accusing the new *rezident* of malfeasance, was the beginning of his undoing. It led to a chain reaction of rebuff-anger-rebuff-fury, which triggered KGB interest in him. Eventually that in turn resulted in the uncovering of his upper-class ancestry.

Progressively cut off by his aberrant behavior from the rewards he considered his due within the Soviet system, he chose to seek recognition elsewhere. No issue of national loyalty ever posed itself for him, any more than it had for Popov. The Soviet government, the Party, the army, the GRU—all these had worth to him only insofar as they honored Oleg Penkovsky. When they no longer achieved this goal they were contemptible and should be destroyed. It was but one simple step further to seeing himself as the savior of the world, and a new messiah was quickly born.

The inevitability of Penkovsky's self-destruction stemmed from the fact that the needs of his ego could never be satiated. "Sir Richard" was sufficient for the moment, but then he wanted recognition by Lord Mountbatten and, after him, the Queen and the president of the United States. Even the tragicomic episode of the uniforms did not provide fulfillment. On the contrary, he was still driven to perform wonders, lest center stage no longer be his. Had his dramatic starring role been denied he might have suffered some form of psychological collapse.

Both Washington and London worried constantly about the increasing chances Penkovsky took. There was little they could do to help, however, once the Soviet authorities' doubts were fully aroused, because Penkovsky was beyond control. Even when he was plainly under suspicion, and KGB watchfulness precluded his escape from the Soviet Union, Penkovsky's case officers were virtually reduced to watching helplessly from afar. They tried to slow the pace of his activity, but for his part Penkovsky was still compulsively searching, like Napoleon or Caesar, for new conquests. There is no indication in the Penkovsky file that any decisive attempt was made to brake his foolhardy behavior, or bring an end to his adventure before it was too late. From my later conversations with some of the men who handled his case (both British and American), it appears that they considered him unstoppable.

MIKHAIL

Mikhail's story illustrates what every experienced intelligence officer knows: a great many of those who seek to earn their living by espionage do so for very selfish and shallow reasons. Because of its secrecy, in fact, the intelligence business is a natural hunting ground for opportunists, con artists, even the mentally deranged. Though there are great differences among them, these undesirables have enough qualities in common to justify calling their behavior pattern the

Espionage Syndrome (or E-S, for short).[9]

If the irresponsibility of Mikhail himself seems to have been carried to almost caricatural extremes, this is in some measure because as an illegal he had no on-the-spot supervision and was subject to no systematic social structure that would have imposed conventional norms and values. His basic psychological tendencies were almost certainly present from the beginning of his life, and they merely emerged more clearly than they might otherwise have done because of the total freedom he enjoyed during his assignment as an illegal.

When considering Mikhail's case more carefully one realizes that, like other members of our sample, he was exceptionally dependent on external cues or symbols to reassure him of his own worth. Until he left the Soviet Union these cues had been programmed for him by the social system. As a career officer in the Red Army he lived within the stabilizing framework of his military rank: his uniform with its insignia, his orders and medals, his salary, and, for several years, his position in charge of the Marx-Lenin University. As an illegal, on the other hand, he had to leave behind whatever valid symbols of distinction he had acquired over the years, even to the point of eschewing his precious uniform and decorations and forswearing his native language except in communications with the center. Occasional encouragement via the radio link emanating from Moscow could hardly have compensated for those many deprivations.

E-S personalities are to an unusual degree absorbed by their own personal concerns; they are egocentric or self-centered, as some would say. Partly for this reason they lack firm loyalty except, perhaps, to those who uncritically nurture and reassure them. In extreme cases— and undoubtedly Mikhail was an extreme case—they lack the ability to love; patriotism and honor are foreign to them. In my view both the personal and official relationships of an E-S personality are governed by a "trigger mechanism" that turns the emotions on and off. An ego-damaging encounter with a superior, for example, could in itself be enough to trigger disloyalty.

One is reminded of Penkovsky's fury at being replaced in Turkey by a general, even though he had known from the beginning that such a change was going to happen. Does that mean he was an E-S personality? No, not in the full sense of the term, because his devotion to Britain and the United States was genuine. Yet within his complex personality clear indications of that defect existed, as they did in varying degrees in all the other Soviet agents I have studied. Mikhail's experience was totally at variance from that of Popov and Penkovsky, both of whom received a good deal of assistance and advice from people they liked and trusted. Moreover, they were given goals that were sensible and achievable. Mikhail was not.

Once in Paris after years of rigid discipline within the Soviet Union, Mikhail's closest direct Soviet superior was thereafter located thousands of miles away, in the Moscow GRU center. His supervisor, probably a fellow colonel, was totally at the mercy of what Mikhail wanted to tell or not to tell him. Therein lay another pitfall: because many E-S–afflicted persons are heavily dependent on the opinions of others, they may become accomplished role players—in effect con men who adjust their apparent personality to suit the audience. This situation makes both their failings and feelings difficult to detect—as those of that seeming pillar of the establishment, Penkovsky, were by such good and loyal friends as Serov and Varentsov. If Penkovsky could deceive such giants as they, imagine the vulnerability of Mikhail's hapless colonel in the center!

Another crucial aspect of Mikhail's life abroad was that he at first felt little or no financial pressures. At the beginning the GRU had provided him with a large sum to cover his official expenses, and he did not hesitate to draw heavily on it to pay for such "operations" as the entertainment of his casual paramours. His motive in eventually establishing an American connection, then, was his need to supplement the sums Moscow provided because both his sexual adventures and practical misadventures had become very expensive. Significantly he seems never to have thought of economizing; the world was made for him, not he for the world.

If Mikhail lost all sense of duty once he was no longer under direct supervision, did he become slovenly in other respects? Superficially, no. In appearance he always remained meticulous about his dress and kept his weight low, in part perhaps because these attributes were the peacock feathers that kept him attractive to the opposite sex. To the average Frenchman, on the other hand, he had little to offer, which made him useless as an intelligence agent. Despite having headed the Marx-Lenin University, he was anything but intellectual; there is no indication in his file of his even reading a newspaper, and he would not have known enough to discuss commerce or finance with a French businessman or politics with a government official. It appears he was untouched by any interest in such serious matters.

Had he been in direct contact with an operationally knowledge-able GRU superior in Paris he probably would have been instructed to get to know military people of various nationalities, particularly Americans. Though the desirability of such an initiative should have been self-evident to anyone trained in intelligence, however, it appears never to have entered his thoughts. He was guided more by his glands than his mind so, as we know, all his potential "agents" were eroto-genic young women utterly useless in the context of his GRU mission.

The difficulty of his assignment is not what prevented him from achieving something practical. Under similar circumstances one can easily imagine Penkovsky's becoming a millionaire. Mikhail's world, on the other hand, had always been one of empty words, of abstract political concepts, of ideology. His absolute lack of apparent ties of affection or loyalty to any individual person or country, his cultural rootlessness, his lack of empathy or understanding of others' feel-ings—all these debilities left him stripped of everything except greed and lust. Despite his failings, however, Mikhail is far from being irrelevant to this study of espionage. Indeed he clearly fits into a category for which psychologists have many names, including antisocial personality, psychopathic personality, and (most succinctly) sociopath. Regrettably, this condition may be a genetically based debility, one for which the only remedy is probably exactly the kind of rigid discipline which Mikhail was deprived of when he went from regular military duty to his assignment as an illegal.

From the welter of conflicting views regarding Mikhail's abnormality one might be content with the definition of the "antisocial personality" provided by the American Psychological Association in 1952: "This term refers to chronically anti-social individuals who are always in trouble, profiting neither from experience nor punishment, and maintaining no real loyalties to any person, group, or code. They are frequently callused and hedonistic, showing marked emotional immaturity, with lack of sense of responsibility, lack of judgment, and an ability to rationalize their behavior so that it appears warranted, reasonable, and justified."[10]

The concept of the antisocial personality is valuable because in varying degrees its accompanying traits may be found in many spies or would-be spies. Anyone who served in the intelligence business overseas in the early days after World War II can remember the merchants who pandered to the wants of frustrated intelligence officers. For example, all our ostensible intelligence on North Korea was either the work of fabricators or of the North Korean intelligence service itself. There is, of course, far too much sophistication in most of the world's intelligence agencies for such a situation to prevail today, yet anyone dealing with secret information collection must nonetheless always be on guard against fabrication supplied by con men or "disinformation" funneled to the West by hostile intelligence agencies.

YURI NOSENKO

Yuri Nosenko is now an American citizen—a good one, I am sure—

and has worked for the U.S. government since his long torment ended. It might, therefore, be considered an inappropriate invasion of his privacy to say anything more, except to wish him well. He deserves every happiness after what he unjustifiably suffered at the hands of some overzealous CIA officers.

PROFILE OF THE AGENT-IN-PLACE

In addition to Popov, Penkovsky, Nosenko, and Mikhail, I studied in depth a number of other cases. Security considerations, of course, have precluded my use of cases that were active at the time. I am not free to use the true names of other members of my comparison group, but respectively have designated them as Sergei, Vladimir, Nikolai, Georgi, Alexei, and Dmitri. In most of these and other cases too little personality information existed to make possible the sort of intensive study accorded my principal subjects. All of these men, however, were born around the end of World War I. No women were included because in that generation the concept of equality of the sexes did not extend to the field of Soviet espionage.

Only one of the agents, Georgi, was a civilian; four were or had been GRU colonels; one was a KGB colonel. All five colonels had spent some time abroad and, with one exception, their intelligence affiliations were disguised with the cover of official positions such as military attaché. In two of these six cases the record of the subjects' youth is so sketchy that I cannot judge what effect the parents or senior siblings had on them. Of the four other men whose histories were somewhat more adequate in terms of personality data, three were orphans or semi-orphans and another had gone on record as having felt unloved at home. Popov's elder brother thus provides an exceptional example of close family guidance.

Intelligence

On the basis of their performances both before and after the agency came to know them, five of the agents certainly possessed above-aver-

age intelligence. Only one of them, Dmitri, may have had an IQ somewhat below average, but all my judgments of him are complicated by
his severe personality difficulties.

Self-expression

All subjects were highly articulate and enjoyed generalizing about
international affairs. Dmitri, for example, felt "quite strongly that
Red China constitutes a political and racial danger to the White
World, and that the USSR and the USA should reach an accommoda-
tion in order that they might confront this danger together." He, however, showed "no disposition to defend with intensity and conviction
any opinion when he was challenged." On the other hand the agents
were frequently laconic and sometimes outright unresponsive when
subjected to detailed and orderly questioning about their backgrounds, unless that process was surrounded by repeated demonstra-
tions of high regard and personal liking. It was obvious that what the
CIA considered a normal and inoffensive part of its duties was misin-
terpreted by these Soviets, to whom even routine questioning about
their personal backgrounds seemed analogous to hostile KGB interrogation.

Appearance

In appearance all men were dignified. Highly conscious of what they
should wear, they dressed conservatively and with great care. They
were also scrupulous about other aspects of their grooming, paying
great attention, for example, to the appearance of their nails and hair.
For all of them personal appearance was obviously closely connected
with social status.

Self-control

Most of the time the agents had themselves good outward control and
appeared to conform to the model demanded by the regime. One of
them, Dmitri, initially seemed to be free of signs of tension but later
showed evidence of being inwardly extremely tense; his behavior

eventually proved aberrant and impulsive.

Self-confidence

Closely related to the agents' outward self-control was another factor: self-confidence. For the most part their level of self-confidence appeared high—often unrealistically so. The agents' seeming sense of immortality led them to take chances that in many cases caught up with them later. They then would invariably react with tension, depression, and pleas for case officer help.

In all cases except one there were pronounced cyclical ups and downs in their self-confidence, usually related to real or fancied slights, such as failure to be promoted, decorated, and so forth. The one seeming exception, Nikolai, a GRU colonel and *rezident,* was so rigidly self-controlled that I know almost nothing about his inner feelings. Only later did we learn that he was under the most severe tension of any of the six.

Ambition

With the exception of Mikhail, all the agents were to some degree ambitious. Their effectiveness in achieving their ambitions, however, varied widely. The most capable of the group, Penkovsky, was blocked by his ancestry and his aberrant behavior in Turkey. Another capable individual, Georgi, the only civilian among the comparison group, was prevented from advancing by lack of headroom in his relatively static government department. In contrast to most other Soviets, however, all these men had already achieved considerable success by the time they came to the agency's attention. Their achievements did not satisfy them for long, however; and they all craved ever-higher ranks and ever-more elaborate expressions of appreciation from their superiors.

Attitude toward Other Soviet Officials

All the agents were extremely conscious of rank. Except for Popov and Dmitri, all came from educated urban families that by U.S. standards would be considered middle or upper middle class. They looked down on fellow Soviets who, regardless of rank, behaved in ways that were *nekulturniy*—a frequently used Russian word most easily translated as "uncultured" but which covers every imaginable social infraction including crudeness in speech or comportment. Khrushchev, for example, was anathema to the military members of our comparison group, not just as a result of his treatment of the army but because of his "lower-class behavior."

Though they may have seemed in many respects quite similar, each of the agents professed to believe that he himself was in some way superior to his colleagues—more intelligent, more highly motivated, or perhaps simply more honest. Indeed, each despised many of his peers and denigrated them regularly.

Loyalties

While each of the agents considered himself a "good Russian," only one of them seems to have developed any feeling of loyalty to the Soviet state. For the others the question of political loyalty simply did not arise, either consciously or unconsciously. They were *not* loyal and, in speaking to Americans, felt no need for pretense; this was probably one of the reasons they could so easily relax in talking to outsiders.

The major exception, Nikolai, was an intense, rigidly self-controlled person who eventually reached very high military rank yet was apparently a prey throughout his career to strong internal conflicts regarding his own political loyalty. To his homeland, Russia, yes, he was loyal in the abstract. But to the Communist state he was not; quite the contrary. The dilemma he faced is obvious, and as a result of not being able to reconcile his own conflicting feelings he vacillated between cooperating fully with the CIA and refusing to cooperate at all. When he was good he was very, very good, but one could never be sure how long that situation would continue.

On the other hand, all the agents professed devotion to their families, but in a rather obscure, conceptual way. I knew that in

Dmitri's order of priorities his career took precedence over his wife. He only infrequently mentioned her as a consideration in his plans. Furthermore, his references to his sons were infrequent. In sum he seemed concerned for the well-being of his wife and sons but lacked strong emotional involvement or dedication to their happiness. Four of the six agents were known to be unfaithful to their wives on a regular basis. Concerning the other two I have no information in this regard. Of those consistently unfaithful, however, only Popov developed a lasting attachment to his mistress.

Did they feel anything akin to loyalty? It would appear so, because there is no record of any of them ever endangering the lives of the foreigners they worked with, even when these agents' own careers and lives were in jeopardy. Thus in effect they displayed more consideration for their foreign contacts than for their own families, some of whom suffered severely when their relatives were unmasked by the KGB—a danger that was always real but one they gave little attention.

Self-indulgence; Attitude toward Money and Possessions

Though I believe all the agents were fundamentally self-indulgent, the group varied widely in the degree to which they were able to control their impulses. Georgi would be very business-like, hard-working, and self-disciplined for long periods of time; his self-control would then suddenly collapse and he would go on a drinking spree, pick up a woman, and squander large sums before sobering up. Conversely Nikolai, the most self-disciplined of the group, manifested no interest in sensual pleasures but did ask for presents of certain items which he himself could not have afforded. These gifts were never, however, incommensurate with the valuable services he rendered.

With the possible exception of Nikolai, the agents all had difficulty in handling money properly, and none could resist living beyond his means. Yet while they enjoyed spending money (frequently for trivial purposes), they were not at all preoccupied with the idea of wealth. The amounts they received from the CIA were insignificant in relation to the risks they took.

Alcohol

Contrary to the stereotype of Russians, none of the Soviet military officers in our sample drank heavily; by present-day U.S. standards they would have been considered moderate social drinkers. One agent drank quite heavily during the period when he was contemplating defection. I do not know, however, how much he consumed under more normal circumstances. Georgi, the civilian, would drink to excess from time to time, but he would also have long periods when he refused all alcohol.

In the course of his trial Penkovsky was forced to testify to his own "moral decay, caused by almost daily use of alcoholic beverages." On one occasion at the Moskva Hotel he said, "I remember having drunk half a liter of cognac." This was all nonsense fabricated by the prosecution, which did not want the ideological reasons for his anti-Soviet activities made public.

In many cases I believe our own agency case officers drank more than their agents did and may actually have encouraged the agents to drink when they would not otherwise have done so.

Physical Condition

None of the agents participated in sports except insofar as their lives were regimented and exercise was required. All were somewhat paunchy except for Mikhail, who prided himself on his athletic achievements as a young man.

As a Moth to a Flame

Everyone in my sample was at various times outside the Soviet Union for substantial periods but, with the exception of Nosenko, none chose to attempt escape until it was too late. Even Mikhail, who became nothing more than a feckless womanizer, went home when summoned. Why?

One of the uniformities that I noted among the men I studied is that none was truly scholarly, religious, or politically oriented. It was certainly not culture, faith, or ideological fealty that took them all back home despite their opportunities to escape. Yet search as one may, it is difficult to find any rationale behind their willingness to return to the USSR. (Even the sophisticated Penkovsky had three opportunities to quit his country for good but elected on each occasion to go back.) I tried to distinguish the individual motivations of some of them in returning to the Soviet Union, despite the obvious threat of KGB discovery and the virtual impossibility of escape.

In my opinion the answer in Penkovsky's case is relatively simple: vengeance was the sustenance of his life and he could not wreak it from afar. His project for an atomic attack on his own homeland showed the depth of his hatred, and he took too seriously for his own good his mission as a soldier of "his" queen and president.

Nikolai, the rigid military man, was highly successful even while vacillating between loyalty and treason. He had several prolonged tours of duty abroad but never took advantage of them to defect, perhaps due to pride on one hand and, on the other, the very fact that he was too inflexible to modify his life by abandoning his native country.

As to Popov, his lack of imagination was such that, when the possibility of escape and emigration was urged upon him in Berlin, he strongly resisted the idea. Despite his army rank to the end he remained a Russian peasant and could not imagine himself functioning on his own in the Western world for the remainder of his life. "Everything will be all right!" he often remarked, because optimism was the only answer he could muster when faced with a dilemma as complex as that posed by the possibility of overt defection and flight.

Dmitri was probably too heavily stressed to be analytical about anything. His rational control was so tenuous that his actions were difficult to assess. One can conjecture that, like Mikhail, he simply conformed to an ingrained pattern by returning home. Concerning

Georgi's last days I cannot remember enough to make a judgment.

Finally, what about Mikhail? Mikhail was a completely bogus intellectual, possessing the Pavlovian reactions of an incontinent dog. When the master whistled, he returned home. When I first considered his case he seemed unimportant, yet he epitomizes most aspects of the Espionage Syndrome.

Though the views of professional psychologists may be helpful in our survey, little psychological literature has been devoted to the study of spies. One can conjecture, nonetheless, that those specializing in psychological abnormality might consider spying a subcategory of the so-called "sociopathic or psychopathic personality." Let me quote briefly from one authority on this subject: "[The sociopath, or antisocial personality] cannot accept things as they are; he is unable to fit into the life of the herd, but tends to lead an independent, individualistic type of existence with no thought of or feeling for his family, his friends, or his country. With all his faults, he may prove very charming, but [as he feels his attraction diminishing] bewilderment, pity, and alarm arise."[11] The sociopath notoriously lacks the ability to foresee the consequences of his own actions, and in many cases seems not even to experience fear. Certain individuals decorated as war heroes for showing enormous courage in combat came to grief after the end of World War II as a result of violent or unscrupulous behavior. Diagnosed as "sociopaths," the origin of their behavioral disorder is controversial and may even be genetic. Because the term is by implication derogatory, I have used it as sparingly as possible. Unusual social factors seem to have combined, probably along with genetic inheritance, to make our subjects what they were. The term Espionage Syndrome provides a distinct and less pejorative behavioral category than those available to psychiatrists.

In sum, despite their shortcomings the people presented here might well have turned into fine citizens, as Yuri did, had they also in the end been liberated from the Soviet spiderweb of their day.

Epilogue
My Soviet Friends

During my CIA career one of the most pleasant surprises was the ease with which I seemed able to make friends with Soviet diplomats abroad. Colleagues of mine, both American and foreign, who had served in Moscow and elsewhere tended to emphasize the difficulties they encountered in establishing anything more than formal business-related contacts with Soviet officials—even those whose job it was to deal with representatives of the non-Communist West in an official capacity. Especially in their own capital, I was told, they were extremely cautious about any contacts not in the official line of duty.

I was naive enough to take for granted that the same difficulties existed outside the Soviet Union; in the strongly anti-Communist nations where I had served in the early years after World War II such was certainly the case. On the other hand, my experience during the early 1960s in Morocco, a country carefully balanced both politically and economically between East and West, was a revelation. To my delight, establishing cordial contact with Soviets turned out to be relatively easy.

Let it be said that those in Rabat, the capital of Morocco,

undoubtedly knew from the beginning that I was the CIA chief and therefore of more than marginal interest to them. I, on the other hand, had been armed with reliable information as to who the KGB representatives were in the Soviet embassy there, and it was they on whom I concentrated my own attention. (I made no effort in regard to the GRU representatives because they appeared interested only in foreign uniformed personnel.) The character of Rabat helped immensely. It was an attractive, modern city, large enough to accommodate the amenities of civilization but small enough for all of us to be neighbors. Situated on the Atlantic coast, the city's broad streets were lined with palm trees, wide sidewalks, and fine single-family dwellings. At a time when countries all over the world seemed to feel duty-bound to establish some sort of presence in a rapidly decolonizing Africa, it is no wonder that Rabat became the preferred choice of many governments as the site of their initial diplomatic representation on that continent. The Soviet official presence in Rabat was particularly noticeable, its size stemming in part from an effort to monitor the large system of U.S. Air Force and Navy bases established in Morocco as part of NATO's military infrastructure.

Yet no one was on edge in this calm and very civilized spot with beaches washed by the mellow waters of the Mediterranean and mid-Atlantic. The subject of potential world conflict seemed as distant as the north and south poles, and when I chatted with Soviets we quickly found enough common interests to be able to skirt subjects that might divide us. One of my favorite Soviets, a senior KGB officer whom I shall call Leo, served as his country's chargé d'affaires for nearly a year, yet as acting chief of the Soviet mission he and his wife seemed much happier enjoying a family dinner with us than they did when I encountered them on more formal occasions. We attended many of the latter, and among the most popular were the National Day celebrations at Rabat's fifty or more embassies. Leo was frank in saying that he dreaded such ceremonies, whereas he found things in our house different. Both he and his wife were fluent in French, our conversations never flagged, and he was frank to a fault—far more than one expected of a senior diplomat. For example, he had served in Egypt before coming to Morocco, but when I posed a pro forma question as to whether he enjoyed the Arabs, he dismissed the idea with a brisk wave of his hand. "Not a civilized people!" he grunted, and his wife, a normally cheerful person, mirrored her husband's feelings by shaking her head and for a moment looking glum.

The four of us had many long talks, and I found him willing to discuss almost anything except the Soviet political system. He seemed happiest when we sat cross-legged on the floor, whisky in hand, to listen to my collection of recorded Russian songs and choral music. At times he would sway, hum, and even sing some of the words—while I confined myself to swaying and humming.

"You must learn the words!" he said on one occasion.

"But I don't know Russian," I replied.

"Never mind. You can memorize. I will send you some records!" Sure enough, when he and his wife returned from a visit to Moscow he brought me a number of fine recordings to supplement my own collection—of pure, simple music, and not as I at first feared of the Russian language, which I had no time to learn.

I became particularly well acquainted with three other Soviet diplomatic families , and like Leo all of them associated with the KGB. They visited our house for dinner, sometimes with other Americans present, and we occasionally even went on picnics together. All were delightful, well-educated people; I remember one of the men telling me that he had hesitated between a diplomatic career and becoming a violinist. To explain his eventual choice he said, "I decided I wanted to see the world!"

Rather strikingly, however, though these Soviets came to our house, they never reciprocated by inviting us to their homes. My wife and I decided this might simply have been because they felt unable to entertain in the same style as we; a generous U.S. government allowed us to bring to our post many personal possessions which Soviet citizens probably could not match.

Nevertheless, that they were sincere friends was later attested to by a singularly kind gesture. Having been sent home from Rabat for medical treatment in Boston, I heard the phone jangle noisily beside my hospital bed early one morning. On the other end was an excited voice speaking from the CIA headquarters in Washington. "John!" the caller said, "we've gotten a cable from our embassy in Algiers saying that your Russian violinist pal [who had by now been transferred to Algeria] contacted them and asked them to express his condolences and warmest wishes for your speedy recovery. He seemed very concerned." Then the agency man quickly slipped back into his ominous professional mode. "You know, of course, that he's KGB, don't you?"

Did I try to recruit for intelligence purposes any of the Soviet officials whom I met in Morocco? Wasn't that what I was there to do? Certainly that was a key part of my job. Yet a mature intelligence officer is one who understands the difference between the possible and the improbable; it is a difficult distinction learned only by experience—and, regrettably, sometimes never learned at all. In any case, none of my local Soviet friends had any of the qualities that distinguished the unhappy men with whom the reader has become acquainted. None of these diplomats in Rabat was a maladjusted peasant like Popov, nor were any of them bitter, frustrated aristocrats who, feeling shorn of their heritage, exploited the Soviet system to the full while doing their best to subvert it; none seemed to partake of Penkovsky's double nature. None were anywhere near the obvious sociopath that Mikhail was, a man whom any intelligent person—particularly his lofty GRU bosses in Moscow—should have been able to assess as completely inadequate. My Soviet friends resembled Yuri least of all. He was the product of an arriviste segment of his nation that lacked tradition and structure and who therefore grew up utterly without loyalty to anyone or anything Soviet, whether family, friends, or country. It was plain that all my acquaintances were, by contrast, well adjusted within their society and therefore had no need to escape it.

Perhaps there were Popovs and Penkovskys among the Soviets in Morocco, but if they existed I never met them. I thus left the country having immensely enjoyed my long stay there, but unable to realize my most cherished professional dream of recruiting a high-level Soviet agent. Moreover, as the temperature of the Cold War became more moderate, a number of my colleagues had similar experiences. The Soviets they met were also agreeable and sociable, but not recruitable.

THE DANGERS OF A WORLD OUT OF BALANCE

Experiences like the ones described in these pages, when taken together with the collapse of the Soviet Union and the emergence of a new Russia as a potential ally of the West, give rise to a challenging question: Will espionage targeted against the former Soviet empire be considered necessary in the future? What was once secret in the old Communist monolith is openly discussed, travel abroad is free, and discussion is relatively unrestricted. The president of Russia is now elected, Russian troops have been evacuated from Eastern Europe, and nuclear weapons previously deployed in Belarus, Kazakhstan, and Ukraine have been returned to Russia. It is tempting to conclude that the threat posed by Russia to the United States and its European allies has changed in character so much as to make espionage an anomaly.

America has, however, learned from bitter experience in the twentieth century to temper its traditional optimism regarding the future. After all, World War I was not the end but the prelude to World War II. The social and economic chaos of Germany and Italy fed rather than dampened nationalist ambitions and territorial expansion. Hopes that the League of Nations might insure peace among the great powers proved to be an illusion. And, while the United Nations was built on a more realistic foundation of cooperation among the great powers, it was ultimately NATO's enormous military strength, backed by a massive global intelligence-collection effort and the nuclear sword of Damocles, that prevented another global holocaust—it was not simply good intentions and the Briand-Kellogg Pact.

With each of its recent military actions—Desert Storm, peace-keeping efforts in the Balkans, and the war in Afghanistan—America has demonstrated more conclusively that it is the sole superpower on the globe. But it is precisely in this disruption of the traditional balance of power in the world that the future threat to America resides. Our seeming monopoly of power breeds envy, insecurity, and fear abroad, while in Washington it tends to beget complacency and an arrogant insensitivity to the interests of other nations. The September 2001 terrorist attack on America was a bitter reminder that the weak use whatever weapons they have at their disposal to challenge the strong.

A weakened Russia may no longer be in a position to challenge America militarily, but Russia, in alliance with other states, can threaten American interests in the future in significant ways. We may also seek Russian cooperation in confronting what may prove to be much more serious dangers to our mutual national interests posed by China, India, or an amorphous global terrorist network. The sheer size of Russia and its potential as friend to us or as an ally of our enemies ensures that it will remain an important concern of our intelligence community. Even in a cooperative relationship like the one beginning to emerge after the September 2001 terrorist attacks, deep currents of suspicion regarding the ultimate intentions of the other will continue on both sides.

The fact that Russia continues to be a major nuclear power, if no longer a seemingly monolithic nuclear threat, is cause for legitimate Western concern. How secure is the Russian nuclear establishment? Is there a danger of another Chernobyl, or of an unauthorized Russian missile launch against American targets, or of acquisition of Russian nuclear materials or Russian specialists in weapons of mass destruction by either hostile states or a terrorist network?

Before the attack of September 2001 Russian president Vladimir Putin had sought, through demonstratively closer ties with China, India, and other states (including those of Western Europe concerned with American "unilateralism"), to compensate for Russian weakness by convincing Washington that Moscow, in alliance with like-minded states, could still be a force to be reckoned with. He quickly realized, however, that Russia would do much better as a declared full-fledged ally of Washington rather than an impotent carping critic. Putin muted his attacks against American unilateralism and sought to minimize the seriousness of the many issues in dispute between our two countries.

What appeared to be a shift in policy shocked Putin's allies in the defense and security services, who grumbled about one-sided concessions being offered to Washington. Polls showed many Russians were suspicious of America's real intentions. These feelings could fuel a significant rift in relations if Washington is perceived to be consistently ignoring, or trampling on, Russian national interests or if the economic gap between Russia and the West continues to widen. Washington needs always to keep in mind that Putin, by suddenly and dramatically allying himself with his former enemy, has taken a gamble. He must be able to show in concrete terms how this gamble has served Russian national interests. Otherwise, pressure to revert to a more obstructionist policy, focused on building up countervailing strength against American "hegemony," could force a change in Russian strategy that is triggered if not by Putin himself, then by a rival politician.

Among the many and often conflicting priorities being demanded of our hard-pressed intelligence community today, the attitudes among the officials surrounding Putin and of Putin himself remain a matter of grave concern. In the coming years no one wants to be asking "who lost Putin?" or why he was toppled. But measuring attitudes and human motivation is obviously a much more difficult task than measuring order of battle. While a satellite photo can often provide a better estimate of combat readiness of enemy forces than can an observer on the ground, it takes a spy planted in the headquarters of an enemy (or even in a purportedly friendly state) to provide informed judgment regarding political attitudes and leadership stability.

In this new information era intelligence analysts and field operators risk being submerged by data that are often contradictory or even deliberately disseminated to confuse the opposition. Setting priorities among the major collection targets such as China, India, Russia, the terrorist networks, the drug networks, economic and financial trends, or explosive points in the Third World has become a much more complex task than it was during the more orderly era of bipolar confrontation. Neither policymakers nor intelligence analysts are at their best when faced with too many options. In making their policy judgments and decisions they must also deal with a public that is much more widely traveled and better informed than ever before. Indeed, among the greatest heroes of recent wars are the newsmen and camera crews who bring the horrors of war into our living rooms with their commentary and photographs. To be sure, there is no way to show adequately on the television screen the agonizing decision making of diplomats and military commanders. But what the public does see on CNN certainly has an impact on public attitudes and public policy.

One vital task of intelligence is to estimate precisely what conclusions leaders and the publics in target countries draw from the information made available to them. An obsessive concern of the Bush Administration has been to efface the image of American weakness left by Vietnam and Somalia that may have encouraged our enemies to believe that Americans would crumble if subject to pressure. A major priority of the intelligence community since planes flew into the World Trade Center and the Pentagon has been to identify and neutralize leaders and movements around the world that have come to view terrorism against American targets as their secret weapon against American political and economic domination of the world.

I would like to think that if any of them are still alive, the members of the KGB whom I knew in posts abroad, "my Soviet friends," feel that our struggle against global terror is their struggle too. On a personal level, these specialists in espionage seemed quite similar in culture, education, and personal aspirations to their equivalents in the CIA. Thus I was not surprised to see supporters of a more democratic, market-oriented Russia emerging from the cosmopolitan ranks of the KGB. Likewise, we should not have been surprised to find rational, articulate leaders like Gorbachev, Yeltsin, and now Putin coming to power in Russia. Each was shaped by his own experience with the failures of Communism and the need for radical reform if Russia was to become competitive in the modern world.

Yet Russians are the first to remind us of the bitter cycle of their history, of how many times reform in Russia has fallen victim to reaction. Whether it was the enlightened Catherine the Great, the liberal reformer Alexander I, or Nicholas II, each stepped back from serious reform when it appeared to threaten her or his autocratic authority. Lenin, and then Stalin, came to power on the ruins of fumbling efforts to achieve highly centralized but pseudo-democratic government in the mid-nineteenth century. The experiment of mixing the cant of Communism with a quasi-military discipline masking as democracy eventually brought nothing better than dictatorial regimentation and bureaucratic sclerosis. Perhaps the Soviet system was preferable to the chaos into which the Russian empire had slid during World War I. The Soviet system seemed almost to have achieved permanency, at least until a new revolution took place—a revolution fired not by Ideology but by the other two "I's," Information about the outside world and awareness of the Insufficiency of Communism. It is this gap between Russia's aspirations to become a modern civilized society and its institutional and economic weakness that remains a source of inherent instability.

The leaders of Tsarist and Communist Russia both recognized that an elaborate intelligence apparatus was the essential instrument for informing themselves about the state of the nation and protecting themselves against enemies, both foreign and domestic. History shows that their confidence was misplaced. The revolt of Tsar Alexander I's favorite Semyonovsky Guards regiment caught him by surprise, while the comic opera Decembrist revolt of liberal officers also caught Nicholas I off guard and the police could not protect the Liberator Tsar, Alexander II, from assassination by fanatic pan-Slavs. Later on, in his manipulative paranoia, Stalin encouraged his secret police to destroy the cream of the Russian Army on the eve of World War II. Finally, it was the head of the KGB who led the abortive revolt in August 1991 against Gorbachev's efforts at reform of Russia. Now, Putin speaks of establishing a "dictatorship of the Law," but in his reliance on the "power ministries" to run Russia he is very much a traditional Russian leader. I suspect that, regardless of the success or failure of the programs of modernization currently being pushed by the Kremlin, the Russian leaders, whoever they are, will in the future continue to look to their intelligence system to warn them of dangers, real or imaginary.

Espionage is not incompatible with a more open Russian society. Moreover, the country's intelligence effort itself is undergoing a major modification, with the services being refocused against a totally different set of targets. In addition to the traditional military and political targets, the diplomatic and intelligence services have been instructed to aggressively collect relevant information on the economic and industrial techniques that have made the Western world and

Japan so successful. In their efforts at espionage, industrial and otherwise, the Russians will continue to find Americans prepared to sell secrets for money or some sort of psychological revenge on a society that has disappointed them.

By the same token, given the widespread disillusionment among Russians with their economic and social conditions, and with the Byzantine infighting so characteristic of the Russian bureaucracy, the CIA should have even greater opportunities to recruit agents among many different levels of Russian society, including within the Kremlin itself. Even the best agents, however, can have their own axes to grind, so that we must be wary of becoming too dependent on agent analyses of Russian reality.

Those of us who have experienced the last seven decades have been fortunate in seeing progress, albeit in fits and starts, toward a generally more humane and integrated global community. Who would have thought some years ago that we might be speaking seriously of helping our old enemy, Russia, join the World Trade Organization or NATO? Does this mean that we can look forward to a world without spies, at least those operating between Russia and the West? The answer is probably no. Among our cautious statesmen and military men, skepticism is so deeply ingrained that, while continuing to seek verification of good news, they are more likely to believe bad news. Clandestinely gathered intelligence has become such a basic tool of diplomacy and military power that policy leaders would be lost without that resource. In fact, no major nation will believe that other major nations are not spying upon it. Each nation feels, in turn, that it needs not only spies but also spycatchers (such as our FBI) or, in the case of Russia, the State Security Bureau (FSB) to spy upon the spies. For no better reason than that suspicion breeds reciprocal distrust, most major nations are likely to continue to be involved with espionage for the foreseeable future. Even the most successful societies will breed both spies and traitors. Indeed, with the events of

September 2001, intelligence agencies across the world have found a new raison d'être.

Notes

Chapter 1. Pyotr Popov

1. H. Feis, *Between War and Peace* (Princeton: Princeton University Press, 1960), 18. Feis may be correct that those were the orders issued by Eisenhower's headquarters, but they certainly never reached the 385th Infantry Regiment of the U.S. Army's Seventy-sixth Division. I remember watching the remnants of a German division, including many men on crutches and some even supported by military nurses, proudly parade past our headquarters. Our regiment accepted at least ten thousand prisoners, probably many more. After carefully screening out undesirables (such as SS members) we did nothing to prevent the rest from heading westward toward what became West Germany. Before heading west to safety, however, a number of the released German troops walked across Zwickau toward our regimental command post to volunteer for service in the U.S. Army. I talked to a number of these men and found that all of them thought America would go on to fight the Russians, in which case they wanted to help. We had to put a large sign above the entrance to our headquarters proclaiming, in German, that we did not accept volunteers for the war in Japan.

2. Ibid., 276–77.

3. The unfavorable pre-revolutionary connotation of this word implied a wealthy but stingy usurer. In the Stalin era it came to mean any farmer who could afford to hire laborers or own farm machinery. In both cases the term was pejorative.

4. V. D. Samarin, "The Soviet School, 1936–1942," in *Soviet Education,* ed. G. L. Kline (London: Routledge & Paul, 1957), 25–37.

5. J. Erickson, *The Soviet High Command* (New York: Westview, 1984), 639–42.

6. Popov never professed any interest in politics. However, during the postwar period a study of emigrés indicated that 83 percent of the sample cited "exposure to the West" as the major factor that led to their disaffection. Over time Popov was certainly affected by the liberty he experienced in both Austria and Germany. See A. Rossi, *Generational Differences in the Soviet Union* (New York: Arno, 1980), 435.

7. The emphasis is the author's. Popov, of course, had no idea how revealing many of his remarks were.

8. D. E. Murphy, S. A. Kondrashev, and G. Bailey, *Battleground Berlin* (New Haven: Yale University Press, 1997), 267–81.

9. Ibid. See also C. Andrew and O. Gordievsky, *KGB: The Inside Story of Its Foreign Operations from Lenin to Gorbachev* (London: Hodder & Stoughton, 1991), 362; G. Blake, *No Other Choice, An Autobiography* (London: Jonathan Cape, 1990), 210–11; W. Hood, *Mole* (New York: Norton, 1982), 265–66, 308–11, 317; and D. Martin, *Wilderness of Mirrors* (New York: Harper & Row, 1980), 102–3, 112–13.

CHAPTER 2. OLEG PENKOVSKY

1. R. Conquest, *The Great Terror* (London: Macmillan, 1968), 228.

2. A. M. Schlesinger, *A Thousand Days* (Boston: Houghton Mifflin, 1965), 317.

3. Ibid., 499.

4. Ibid., 380.

5. J. E. McSherry, *Khrushchev and Kennedy in Retrospect* (Palo Alto: Open-Door Press, 1971), 73.

6. L. Pistrak, *The Grand Tactician* (New York: Praeger, 1961), 218–19.

7. Here once again Penkovsky was referring to the chiefs of state of Great Britain and the United States, whom he saw as personally, though invisibly, presiding over the secret meetings that had taken place in Britain and France.

8. Quoted in P. Smith, *A New Age Now Begins* (New York: McGraw-Hill, 1976), 17.

9. This observation is at least partially untrue. Kisevalter seems to have forgotten Popov, who had not a single intimate among his fellow Russians.

10. For an interesting analysis see J. L. Schecter and P. S. Deriabin, *The Spy Who Saved the World* (New York: Scribner's, 1992), 402–21.

CHAPTER 3. YURI NOSENKO

1. Another acceptable translation is, "We shall be present at your funeral," but I have used the currently accepted version.

2. On 15 September 1978, as principal witness for the CIA I gave testimony about Nosenko for more than three hours before the U.S. House of Representatives Select Committee on Assassinations.

3. J. P. Zubek, "Behavioral and Physiological Effects of Prolonged Sensory and Perceptual Deprivation: A Review," in *Man in Isolation and Confinement,* ed. J. E. Rasmussen (Chicago: Aldine, 1973), 9–10.

CHAPTER 5. MOTIVATION

1. R. A. Bauer, A. Inkeles, and C. Kluckhohn, *How the Soviet System Works* (Cambridge: Harvard University Press, 1956), 181.

2. Ibid., 182–83.

3. In the intelligence services of any of the U.S. or Allied forces he would have been considered totally inadequate.

4. L. B. Ely, "The Officer Corps," in *The Red Army,* ed. B. H. L. Hart (New York: Harcourt, 1956), 397–98.

5. R. A. Feldmesser, "Persistence of Status Advantages," *American Journal of Sociology* 59 (July 1953): 19–27.

6. A. Inkeles and R. A. Bauer, *The Soviet Citizen* (Cambridge: Harvard University Press, 1959), 75–76.

7. Such forces, of which there were several, were joined by troops from the United States, Great Britain, France, Japan, and others. These Allied units proved ineffective and were eventually evacuated. The White Russian forces were even less fortunate; those not killed were imprisoned and never liberated.

8. From his own childhood as an American abroad, the author remembers a number of Russian emigrés in Europe and the Near East in the late 1920s and early 1930s as still absorbed, many years after the Revolution, with an attending loss of status. Penkovsky's mother had probably hammered into her son tales of the Revolution and his consequent deprivation.

9. Syndrome: "A group of symptoms characteristic of a particular personality pattern or psychological problem." Espionage Syndrome is a term of my own devising that will not be found in any psychological dictionary. Nonetheless, during my intelligence career both my colleagues and I not infrequently found ourselves having to deal with such people.

10. R. M. Goldenson, "Antisocial Reaction," in *The Encyclopedia of Human Behavior,* vol. 1 (New York: Doubleday, 1970), 86.

11. D. K. Henderson, *Psychopathic States* (New York: Norton, 1939), 128–29.

Bibliography

Andrew, C., and O. Gordievsky. *KGB: The Inside Story of Its Foreign Operations from Lenin to Gorbachev*. London: Hodder & Stoughton, 1991.

Bauer, R. A., A. Inkeles, and C. Kluckhohn. *How the Soviet System Works*. Cambridge: Harvard University Press, 1956.

Beier, H., and P. A. Bauer. "Oleg: A Member of the Soviet Golden Youth." *Journal of Abnormal and Social Psychology* 55 (July 1955).

Blake, G. *No Other Choice, An Autobiography*. London: Jonathan Cape, 1990.

Conquest, R. *The Great Terror*. London: Macmillan, 1968.

Ely, L. B. "The Officer Corps." In *The Red Army*, ed. B. H. L. Hart. New York: Harcourt, 1956.

Erickson, J. *The Soviet High Command*. New York: Westview, 1984.

Fainsod, M. *Smolensk under Soviet Rule*. Cambridge: Harvard University Press, 1958.

Feis, H. *Between War and Peace*. Princeton: Princeton University Press, 1960.

Feldmesser, R. A. "The Persistence of Status Advantages in Soviet Russia." *American Journal of Sociology* 59 (July 1953): 19–27.

Goldenson, R. M. "Antisocial Reaction." *The Encyclopedia of Human Behavior.* Vol. 1. New York: Doubleday, 1970.

Henderson, D. K. *Psychopathic States.* New York: Norton, 1939.

Hood, W. *Mole.* New York: Norton, 1982.

Inkeles, A., and R. A. Bauer. *The Soviet Citizen.* Cambridge: Harvard University Press, 1959.

Mangold, T. *Cold Warrior.* New York: Simon & Schuster, 1991.

Martin, D. *Wilderness of Mirrors.* New York: Harper & Row, 1980.

McSherry, J. E. *Khrushchev and Kennedy in Retrospect.* Palo Alto: Open-Door Press, 1971.

Murphy, D. E., S. A. Kondrashev, and G. Bailey. *Battleground Berlin.* New Haven: Yale University Press, 1997.

Pistrak, L. *The Grand Tactician.* New York: Praeger, 1961.

Rossi, A. *Generational Differences in the Soviet Union.* New York: Arno, 1980.

Samarin, V. D. "The Soviet School, 1936–1942." In *Soviet Education,* ed. G. L. Kline. London: Routledge & Paul, 1957. 25–37.

Schecter, J. L., and P. S. Deriabin. *The Spy Who Saved the World.* New York: Scribner's, 1992.

Schlesinger, A. M. *A Thousand Days.* Boston: Houghton Mifflin, 1965.

Smith, P. *A New Age Now Begins.* New York: McGraw-Hill, 1976.

Volin, L. *A Century of Russian Agriculture.* Cambridge: Harvard University Press, 1970.

Zubek, J. P. "Behavioral and Physiological Effects of Prolonged Sensory and Perceptual Deprivation: A Review." In *Man in Isolation and Confinement,* ed. J. E. Rasmussen. Chicago: Aldine, 1973. 9–10.

Index

About the Author

John Limond Hart was born in 1920 in Minneapolis. The son of a White House correspondent turned diplomat, he grew up in Albania and Persia. As a bilingual U.S. Army escort officer he served as an interpreter with the French Second Armored Division when he landed at Normandy in 1944 and ended his military career as a liaison officer with the French occupation forces in Germany. After completing his postwar studies in international relations at the University of Chicago, he joined the CIA's Directorate of Operations in senior posts at headquarters and abroad. As special assistant to Secretary of the Treasury George Schultz, Hart created a modern Office of National Security Affairs and was the treasury representative on the U.S. Intelligence Board. He was twice awarded the Distinguished Intelligence Medal.

Following retirement Hart received a master's in psychology from George Washington University. He later lived in London and Paris, where he did research for a book on Tsar Alexander I, reflecting a lifetime of avid reading and writing. Mr. Hart died in 2002 and is survived by his wife, Katharine.